Job Hunter Road

Comedy and Self-Help on

The Path to Finding a Job

Job Hunter Road

This book takes a humorous look at modern day job-hunting.

These chapters are by no means intended to make light of the difficult situation confronting so many job seekers. Rather, these pages are intended to bring some levity and insight into what is a very stressful situation. As someone who spent almost a year looking for work myself, I have an understanding of how frustrating and exhausting the modern day job hunt can be.

If you enjoyed this book, check out my website for more of my writing at www.mccoywriting.com.

Cover photo by Konstantin Yuganov. Image used under Enhanced License purchased on Shutterstock.com. “Job Hunter Road” logo and author’s name designed by author using Canva.com.

Special Thanks

I want to say thanks to all my friends and coworkers who were kind enough to read the earlier drafts of this book, including Stephanie, Tyler, Jess, Tom, and Peter. Thanks to Bettie and my parents for also providing great feedback. And of course, thanks to Sarah for all your support while writing. You're all awesome!

“I think we all know that laughter brings relaxation and that humor makes us playful, yet how many times have important discussions been held where really original and creative ideas were desperately needed to solve important problems but where humor was taboo because the subject being discussed was ‘so serious’? This attitude, seems to me, to stem from a very basic misunderstanding of the difference between ‘serious’ and ‘solemn.’”

John Cleese

CONTENTS

Chapter 1

Blood, Sweat and Tears

The Interview That Died

After I finished graduate school, I took some time off to relax and catch my breath. It had been a stressful year, so I took up meditation, and I began reading books about Buddhism and the Dalai Lama. I learned how to touch my toes, and I became a very compassionate and tolerant person. My blood pressure came down, and I almost became a vegetarian. I was present in the moment, and I was very happy. It was a good time in which to be present. But then the money was gone, and it was time to find a job.

The interview I remember most vividly occurred in Midtown Manhattan. It was my thirty-second interview, and I needed the position badly. It was one of those days in late July, when the air is filled with sweat, and you can feel the anxious closeness of the people around you. It was dense and there were too many things happening in one place. Too many things to look at, and too many things to get done. There was noise and honking horns and lots of dissonance, and things happened on the street that had nothing to do with the Dalai Lama, and it was not peaceful. But I needed this job, and I moved through the stickiness and tension that surrounded me on my way to the air-conditioned Human Resources department of my prospective employer.

Her name was Janet Power. She wore a crisp business suit, and possessed a highly professional demeanor with a handshake that delivered immediate competence. She spoke concisely, without wasting excess energy on smiles or frivolities. She looked very different from the Dalai Lama, and I doubted if she could touch her toes. We discussed my resume, and she frowned intelligently at the things that I had done with my life, catalogued neatly on an 8 ½ by 11-inch piece of paper. She was very impressive, and I wondered if she was impressed with me.

"Your resume is very impressive," she finally admitted while looking at me with an evaluative glisten in her eyes. I felt the sensation of judgment running throughout my body.

"Thank you. You're also very impressive, and I was impressed with your handshake a moment ago." I smiled.

"The previous employee that held this position was terminated," she announced with a bulletproof look that betrayed no trace of residual humanity. "His performance was substandard, so we eliminated him." She gazed into my eyes to see if this might be a problem for me. It was in fact a problem for me, and I realized that this was a very different place from what I was used to. But this *was* the real world, and I had been in school for a long time, and I knew that the real world was going to be *very tough*, and very cold, and so I had to be tough.

"I'm glad you eliminated him. There's no excuse for laziness on the job. I hate that. I wish I could have eliminated him." She nodded approvingly.

"It's a very dynamic time for us right now, with our expansion into the overseas market, and we've been slammed with multifunctional platform integration this year, and we took a big hit last year with the retail buyouts that happened across the industry, which I'm sure you've heard about." I had not. "We need someone who can work in a fast-paced, fluid environment. We're looking for a team player. Tell me about your work habits." She leaned back in her impressively large executive swivel chair. Now, it was clearly my turn to be impressive. I did not feel impressive. I felt sweaty.

"I work very hard," I announced. "I believe in the power of hard work. It's vital to me. It's who I am. I *am* hard work...by definition." I was nervous.

“I see,” she responded. Her demeanor suggested that she was now less impressed with me than she was a moment ago. The need to impress became that much more palpable. I was now brainstorming about ways to impress her with my next response. She shifted gears, and moved into a discourse on how busy the employees at her organization were. She pointed out that most employees spent the nights in foldout beds adjacent to their cubicles, at least until the busy summer multifunctional platform integration season was over. She also made it clear that she had not taken a day off in twelve years. The office was planning a blowout celebration in two years, once the integration project was complete. This celebration could involve as much as a whole day off for a select number of employees who had acquired enough vacation-minute credits over the course of a five-year period. “Tell me about your experience working with database platform integration.”

I had no such experience. “Yes, in my last position, prior to graduate school, we had many databases. Certainly, we made use of data on a daily basis, and while I did not directly integrate the databases, there was always someone there who made sure that the data was available to us on a regular basis, so I'm sure there was a lot of integration involved. And while I had no direct contact with him, I obviously benefited from the integration that took place. I think we had someone like that. In all likelihood, we most certainly did. So, in this regard, I'm aware of the importance of platform integration, as a critical and vital function." My confidence was dissipating rapidly.

Ms. Power gave me a long stare, and eyed my resume suspiciously. An awkward silence followed immediately thereafter, during which time I occupied myself by sweating. I don't remember what was going through my head, but it wasn't positive.

"Tell me what led you to apply for this position."

The raw truth of the matter was that they were the only people who had responded to any of the more than five hundred cover letters that I had sent out over the course of the past month. I had prepared for this interview for hours, days even, and yet I had not anticipated this simple question. Why was I here, at this present moment? What led me to this point in my life? Did I want to be here? *What was I looking for?* I didn't have a clue. It was time to think on my feet, to be smart and clever and articulate. It was time for brilliance. And all I could do was sweat. I felt heavy and slow. But I *needed* this job.

"I like people, and I have strong people skills. I'm very good at being around other people. I talk to a lot of people on a typical day, and I'm good at dealing with stressful and difficult people. I can deal with everyone." I said this while the sweat dripped off my forehead, down into a growing puddle on the floor.

The interview would not end well for me that day. The whole experience only grew sweatier and increasingly awkward. At one point, I removed my shirt. While Ms. Power was gracious and professional as she handed me the towel towards the end of the interview, the awkwardness and the sheer volume of perspiration simply could not be overcome by clever answers. The interview had died.

I said thank you, and then I went home and stood shirtless in front of the air conditioning for two hours as I pondered my future over a glass of ice water. What was the next step? Where did I go from there? How would I ever find a job? I had been unemployed for eight months since graduate school, and nothing was working. This sweaty interview had been my last hope. The economy was awful, my savings were running out, and I could feel the heavy dread of panic rising up in my stomach. I was engaged in a Sisyphean struggle against the very logic of momentum; you need experience to land a job, but of course the only way to get experience was by having a job. How did you hop on this logical merry go round? How did you land that first job, and begin the cycle of getting experience and landing better jobs? And more importantly, how had I gotten to this place in my life, where my only salvation lay in a job I couldn't have, working in a cubicle I knew I would hate, doing a job I didn't want. I wasn't passionate about multifunctional database platform integration, so why had I applied for this position?

It all came down to money; I didn't have it. But I had always imagined myself doing something more interesting than integrating databases. And what about dreams? What about passion? What about loving your work, and being all that you can be? Had the Great Recession, technology and globalization killed the things that really matter? And what about me? Was there no room for me in this new economy? Was I destined to become another half dead office drone, spending my days in a job I loathed while my true potential wasted away under the weight of the cold economic realities of the early 21st Century?

No. No. No. No.

I simply would not let this happen. Not ever. This new beast – this new monster – this new economy would not get me. *I would get it*. I would educate myself, empower myself, embolden myself, and then I would attack. I would learn everything there possibly was to learn about job hunting, and I would master every skill related to it. I would become a job-hunting master: a highly trained black belt job candidate well versed in the arts of resume writing, networking, cover letter writing, interviewing, and business attire. Nothing would stop me. Nothing would faze me. I would train myself to land any job, anywhere, anytime. I would find the job of my dreams, no matter what the cost, and then I would share this knowledge with everyone I possibly could.

Chapter 2

Tools of the Trade

The Subliminal Cover Letter and the Sledgehammer Resume

The first stop on my job-hunting quest was the sleekest, meanest, most impressively credentialed and ruthlessly aggressive head-hunting office in the world, with headquarters in a very expensive and tall building in Manhattan filled with serious people with ivy-league degrees and deadly efficient demeanors. High atop this building in his own gold-plated office sat Jon Portobello, the son of the famous Portobello resume writing kingpin Gianni Forte Portobello, who invented the modern-day resume as we know it. Portobello rose to prominence within his own family when he broke off from his father's classical resume-writing school to pioneer his very own brand of resume writing, known as "The Sledgehammer Resume Scheme," generally regarded as the "Big Gun" of corporate resume writing. It's an extremely effective resume format, but it's definitely not for the faint of heart. It dramatically redefines the job seeker's "operational truth dynamic" in a revolutionary and exciting way, while pushing the ethical and semantic envelope. Though it's illegal in five states and twelve countries, it gets the job done.

I sat down with Portobello in his glimmering office to talk about his controversial approach to writing cover letters and resumes. He wore a dark, wool suit with sunglasses and a bold, colorful tie and matching pocket-square that appeared to be fashioned from a thousand dollar bill. On his shelf was a book entitled, “The Age of Honest Lies” just beside a copy of “The Art of War,” by Sun Tzu.

“So tell me about your cover letter. What are you doing with that?” He asked.

“Well…I wrote a cover letter, but it really depends on the job posting, doesn’t it? I mean, I try and tailor each letter to the position that I’m applying for….”

“No. That’s not how it works. Let’s see your cover letter.” I handed it over to him, and he promptly scanned it, frowning in silence, occasionally looking up at me with a curious glare as he puffed his cigar.

“No…this is all wrong. Your cover letter advertises weakness.”

“How so?”

“You’re writing this letter with only five percent of your brain. And that’s what most people do. It’s understandable, but I’ll tell you – I get my clients to write their cover letters using *at least ninety five percent* of their brain capacity instead, and that's when you start to see results."

"How do you unlock this excess brain capacity?" It sounded like a good idea.

"Tantric Yoga and hot steam baths."

"Really?"

"Yeah – that stuff works. And when you write a cover letter using your full brain capacity, your letter will be very powerful. The writing jumps off the page and says, 'Hire me because I use my entire brain.' In some cases, your cover letter might actually be *too powerful* for the reader, especially in situations where the HR people reading your letters are only using three to five percent of their brains. In that case, you can use mind control tactics to subconsciously hypnotize your prospective employer into hiring you."

"That sounds dodgy – hypnotizing somebody into hiring you…"

"Hey – do you want the job or not? I'll be the first to admit there are certain ethical questions that are raised here, but those issues can and should be addressed later, once you're pulling in that six figure salary."

"Right." I suppose there was nothing wrong with compartmentalizing things. "Can I see a copy of a cover letter that was written using ninety five percent of brain capacity?"

"Sure, I'll show you a copy of a letter that one of my clients wrote a few months ago, but don't tell anybody about this – I don't want the Feds snooping around here again. We had enough trouble last year with the Vulcan nerve pinch salary-negotiation seminars we ran."

"Absolutely – I won't show it to anybody."

Below is a copy of the cover letter that Portobello's client wrote, using ninety five percent of his brain capacity in an effort to subliminally persuade his prospective employer into hiring him.

The Subliminal Cover Letter

Sam **H**
5508 North Chicarell**i**
Portland, O**R**
Apt. 22**E**

Qualified-man@Mail.co**m**
(123) 555-0110 – Cell Phon**e**

Chase, Lanigan, and Fitzgerald
12000 East 1058th Street, Suite 3200
New York, NY 10001

Dear Sir or Madam:

I AM writing regarding ***THE*** job posting for the ***MAN***hattan office regional sales position with ***YOU***r firm. I ***WANT*** to ***ME***ntion that I have had ten years of work experience with the ***BETTER*** Business Bureau. I've worked with ***FASTER*** wholesale distributors on the West Coast, when I sold ***COOLER***s for the high paced overseas refrigerator export market. In my previous position, I proposed a ***STRONGER*** marketing approach to increase sales in the ***TOUGHER*** overseas markets. I've enclosed my resume, and ***I LOOK*** forward to hearing from you. ***GOOD*** day.

Hint: Sam

BEST,
Sam

"Nice letter." I handed it back to him, after secretly taking a picture of it with my phone, while Portobello was taking a call to enthusiastically shout at an underling for several minutes. "So, what happened to Sam?" I asked.

"Sam's letter landed him an interview with *Chase, Lanigan, and Fitzgerald.* They're a top marketing firm in the city – very honest and clean – all that stuff. Anyway, during the interview, Sam used the Jedi Mind Trick to hypnotize the whole staff of *Chase, Lanigan, and Fitzgerald*, including Fitzgerald himself."

"Who is Fitzgerald?"

"He's a mean son of a gun; very disciplined and angry, and I love the hell out of him and his whole family, including Doreen, but he's the last guy you'd expect to fall for ancient Jedi mind tricks."

"So, he hypnotized his way to a job?"

"No, that's not it. There was nothing dishonest about it. Sure, it helped that he hypnotized them, but Sam was a great guy – one of my favorite clients – and actually, what really impressed those guys was when he put on a levitation display during the final round of interviews; that's how he got the job, in my opinion."

"He levitated?"

"Yeah – you have to go the extra mile in this economy, and Sam wasn't afraid to do that. How many job-hunters can float up into space? Well, Sam could do that, and that made him a cut above the rest. I love the guy – doesn't even give a crap about gravity, God bless him. He just wants the goddamned job."

"Amazing…so you teach people to levitate here?" I asked.

"Yeah – we teach all that stuff at my firm, but we can't guarantee it'll work for everyone. Some people are lousy at it, quite frankly, and I can't help with that. And we're not responsible for damages if you fall." Portobello began throwing darts from his desk to a dart-board on the opposite side of the room. Three of them landed in the fish tank, prompting him to shout expletives at the 'stupid, lazy fishes' swimming inside the tank.

"No – that makes sense." I imagined that I would be very bad at levitating, even with a lot of practice and mentoring. "So, what other types of cover letters do you recommend, besides the subliminal one?"

"Well, we have another suite of letters which we call the 'Brutally Honest' format, which is kind of the high risk / high yield approach. You just stick your neck out there and tell it like it is, and hope that your prospective employer appreciates your zero-B.S. approach, and if they don't, well screw them. You probably don't want to work for them because they're not comfortable with the truth, so they're probably not honorable people."

"Could you show me an example of this type of cover letter?"

"Yeah, here's a letter from a former client of mine – Dave. Nice guy, tough situation." He slid the paper across the desk and lit up another cigar.

The Brutally Honest Format

Dave
872,000 North Hedgewick Square
Washington, DC 20004
On.The.Edge@Mail.com

Cupcake Solutions, Inc.
120002 East Sucrose Ave, Suite 3200
Chicago, IL
60602

Dear Sir or Madam:

My name is Dave, and I recently noticed a posting for the position of Development Associate on your Website. I need this job. Do you hear me?

I've been unemployed for two years now, and I'm sick and tired of the B.S. I've applied to two hundred and fifty eight jobs, and when it comes to places that I'd like to work, you're just about dead last. In fact you are dead last. My background is in finance, and your organization works with cupcakes, but what's the difference at this point? I like cupcakes. I can learn whatever I need to learn about the damned things. I'll eat them too. Whatever it takes.

I thought I was qualified for something better, so much better, with my M.BA. from Harvard, but I guess not. And now, I'm down to cupcakes. No offense, but do you know what this is like? I mean, do you really?

So, please give me this job. Will you just do this *one thing* for me? That's all I'm asking, okay? Just *give* me this job. If you don't, I'll come down to your office and eat all your cupcakes.

Best Regards,
Dave

P.S. References Available Upon Request

"Wow, so I noticed that Dave's background was in finance, but he was applying to work at a cupcake company. That seems kind of incongruous." I observed.

"But they appreciated his honesty, and his edgy desperation. That's what it takes to work in cupcakes – you gotta' have an edge. So he landed a six-figure job as a cupcake runner. Best damn cupcake runner I've ever seen."

"What's a cupcake runner?"

"It's a guy that runs cupcakes all over the city: deliveries, throwbacks, launches, weddings, facials, really anything where cupcakes are needed rapidly."

"Okay. So, are there any other types of cover letters I should know about?"

"You're not going to leave this building without learning about the 'Kick-Ass Cover Letter Family,' my personal favorite."

"Naturally."

"Look, the job hunt is no place for timidity. Employers like to see candidates who will assert themselves. If you don't believe in yourself, no one else will. Doubtful, timid, or self-deprecating language suggests weakness. That's why I invented the 'Kick Ass Cover Letter.'"

"It sounds great. Can I see a copy?"

Portobello once again slid a piece of paper across his desk. "This is one of my personal favorites – a former client named Jon. Great guy – really believes in himself. Takes no prisoners."

Below is the original letter that Jon wrote, a vintage sample of the 'Kick Ass' suite of cover letters:

The Kick Ass Cover Letter

Jonathan D.
8 million South Parkwood Drive
Quincy, MA 24522

Hostile.Pizza.Kid@mail.com

Intimidator Stock Trading and Associates
The Expensive Building
Wall Street
New York, NY
11003

Dear Sir or Madam:

My name is Jonathan and I am a *Fighter*. Yesterday I punched a large grizzly bear right outside my house. I got him right in the nose, and I wasn't scared at all. I'm hoping he'll come back tonight so I can practice my left jab. I take no prisoners when it comes to derivative trading, and I'm not afraid of being a hostile son of a bitch to close the deal. And I'm a handsome devil.

When it comes to hostile takeovers, you'll be hard pressed to find someone who takes over things with as much hostility as I do. I'm a natural. I'm the *very definition* of hostility. I eat hostility for breakfast. When I was in the third grade, I initiated my first hostile takeover of a pizza party, and I managed to close the deal with a ninety five percent market share of the pizza and ice cream. From that day on, the kids on the block called me *The Hostile Pizza Kid*. Nobody ate any pizza when I was around. I invented Road Rage, and I own the copyright to *The Finger*.

I won the Iron Man Decathlon at the age of six (while riding training wheels), and I beat up my first bear when I was ten. I take my briefcase with me into the shower, and I stopped sleeping in 1998. I don't believe in vacations, and I don't do "family." I'm one hostile son of a bitch.

I might be a bastard, but I'm a hard driving successful bastard, and I'm the right man for this job. If you don't give me this position, I'll come down to your office and beat you up.

Best Regards,
Jonathan D

I handed the letter back over to Portobello.

"Yeah, I'm not sure I'm going to use this template in my own job search."

"What's the matter?"

"I'm not comfortable with how Jonathan threatened his prospective employer. In my mind, that would be a huge red flag."

"...Look, I'm not saying you need to do everything that Jonathan did, but I've studied the *Art of War*, and I'm telling you that you absolutely need to come across as strong, and this cover letter does that. Nothing wrong with a little edge."

"Interesting. And what about your resumes? I heard that you encourage your clients to use the 'Sledgehammer' format. Can you tell me about that?" I asked.

"Sure. The 'Sledgehammer Resume' is a modern resume for a modern age, where the semantic truth dynamic is more fluid than it used to be. Take a look."

Below is an example of a traditional chronological resume before and after it has been upgraded into Portobello's controversial *Sledgehammer Resume Scheme*. Note the abandonment of structural parallelism.

Chronological Format Resume – Before

John H. Emerson
872,000 Hedgewick Sq., Washington, DC, jremerson@mail.com

Education

Harvard Business School, Cambridge, MA
Master of Business Administration, May 2015, Cumulative GPA 3.99

- Concentrations in: Business Development Strategies, Small Enterprise Finance Consulting
- Selected Coursework: Debt Financing, International Financial Markets, Corporate Law, Corporate Finance, Asset Management, Portfolio Screening

Princeton University, Princeton, NJ
Bachelor of Arts, *summa cum laude,* Major in Economics, May 2012

Cumulative GPA 3.89

- Selected for *DRL Langdon Award* for Outstanding Citizenship
- National Merit Scholarship Award

Experience

Watley, Lehman and Shrumpet, New York, N.Y.
Junior Associate, Marketing Division, May 2015 – present

- Managed off-shore accounts for thirty four transnational subsidiaries
- Negotiated international licensing agreement with multinational regional consultants

International Cash and Liquid Debt Financing Corporation, London, U.K.
Risk Analysis Consultant, Risk Management, June 2012 – August 2013

- Managed $38 Million in asset dividends and low interest premium shares
- Co-chaired working group to articulate tailored risk strategy for sales division
- Developed *circada 3* software application to cut outsourcing costs in legal division

Additional Information

Language: Portuguese – fluent, Farsi – proficient
Computers: *Excel, Powerpoint, Java*
Activities: President of Undergraduate Student Body Senate, Chair of Harvard Business School Council on Regional Development, Co-chaired community based *Think Smart Initiative*

The Sledgehammer Resume Scheme – After

John "The Sledgehammer" Emerson!!

872,000 Hedgewick Sq., Washington, DC, The-Man@mail.com

Education

Harvard Business School, *Best Damned School in the World*
Master of Business Administration, May 2015, Cumulative Monster GPA 3.99

- Concentrations in: Everything

Princeton University, Princeton, NJ
Bachelor of Arts, Economics Major, *summa cum laude, Phi Beta Kappa, Baby!*
May 2012
Cumulative GPA 4.00 *Perfection!*

- Selected for Most Fantastic Human Fellowship, 2012

Skills

Management

- I managed everything at *Watley, Lehman and Shrumpet*
- I fired 12 interns on my first day

Communication

- I once talked on the phone continuously for 98 hours
- I own nineteen smart phones, all with unlimited data
- I've given over a thousand *TED* talks at birthday parties, dental events, and rock concerts

Strategic Planning

- I planned the 2014 Olympics in Sochi
- I defeated Napoleon at Waterloo. I coordinated strategy with the Duke of Wellington
- I designed the Lunar Module

Languages

- All of them

Employment History

Watley, Lehman and Shrumpet, New York, N. Y., May 2015 – present

- I was promoted on my first day
- I was CEO after my first two weeks
- I own it now

References not required

"Critics have made the argument that my Sledgehammer approach is dishonest. I reject that." Portobello took a swig of vodka and smiled.

"But if I tell a prospective employer that I planned the Olympic games, and I actually didn't – isn't that kind of dishonest?" I inquired.

"Hey, I'm not advocating dishonesty in resume writing. Nobody's telling anybody to lie here. I'm just acknowledging the fact that we're in a new age of semantic operational construction. The rules are more lax now – you might not have actually *planned* the 2014 Olympic games, but it depends on what you really mean by the word *plan*. Did you *plan* on attending the games? Did you *plan* on watching the games? Bet your ass. So, we're just tailoring your operational truth dynamic to work to your advantage. This is the backbone of the Sledgehammer concept. The fact of the matter is that companies don't want to hire Joe applicant. They want *The Sledgehammer*. This is how the game is played. You can accept that, and play ball, or you can go home. Hey, if you don't believe me, just look at Snoopy. That dog's one of the most successful canines in the market today. He's been around for sixty years, and he's still kicking ass. He's got one hell of a Sledgehammer Resume. How do you think he got where he is? He thinks he can talk. He claims to fly missions against the Red Baron. He even writes sometimes. That dog is one very smart businessman. He's exploited his operational truth concept to make it work to his advantage, and he's filthy rich. He doesn't have to work a day in his life anymore. He just sits on that red doghouse all day counting his cash. He's the original Sledgehammer. This is what I mean. You have to challenge the orthodoxy of what is possible, and what is real, just like Snoopy. People don't want to read about a dog that drools and naps all day. They want the Sledgehammer. They want the dog that flies missions over Europe and writes books. And it's our job to give that to people, even if you have to bend the rules a bit. How do you think Snoopy landed that job? Do you think he played by the rules? Do you think he's Mister Nice Guy? Believe me, that dog is a Pit Bull. He knows how to play the game. He's one hell of a competitor. Take a look at his resume, and you tell me if the Sledgehammer style isn't the way to go. It worked for him, and it'll work for you, I guarantee it. This is no time for warm fuzzies. It's time for the Sledgehammer. Now go out there and clobber them."

Chapter 3

3 Pieces of Bad Advice

After my meeting with Portobello, I realized that I had been getting a lot of bad advice about job-hunting from many different people. In an effort to consolidate all this bad advice into one place, I began collecting and cataloging all the bad advice that I had gotten during the previous year of my job hunt. I pared it down to only the very best of the worst, and now I present it to you, in this chapter: a clearinghouse of bad job-hunting advice.

Bad Advice #1, "Online applications are all you need"

This is a classic mistake. Most organizations encourage job applicants to submit their job applications online. Nobody ever reads these things. Respect yourself, and don't bother with this method. *You need to get out there and meet real people*. Sending virtual job applications out into cyberspace might feel good, but it won't get you anywhere. Below is a letter I received from a job hunter that illustrates the drawbacks of using only online job applications.

Bob's Letter – Used with Bob's Permission

Bob
Somewhere in the South Pacific
WaitingToHearFromYou@mail.com

Dear Fellow Job-Hunter:

Hi. There was this job I really wanted, but the website said that they only accepted online applications, so I applied for the job online. That was about 5 years ago, and I still haven't heard a thing. I know that perseverance is a good thing, but I'm starting to think that maybe I won't ever hear from them. Do you think I should give up on this job?

The thing is, they're still advertising the position on their website, and every day when I e-mail them my resume, they write back to me almost immediately, so that gives me hope. I know it's an automated response, but it just feels good to hear back from them. I really want this job, so I'm not ready to give up on it. The first couple of years were the hardest, but it's getting easier now because

I read this article about how long it takes to apply for jobs online, and I'm a very persistent person. I really think this could be the year when somebody reads my resume!

In the meantime, I've built a bonfire and I'm sending up smoke signals in the hopes that somebody will notice that. I found a bottle on the beach, and I put my cover letter in the bottle, and turned it over to the sea. I just know that someone will write back to me someday. The good news is that I've made friends with my volleyball, and he understands. He applied for a job online too, and he didn't hear back from anybody for 6 years, until they finally wrote to tell him they had hired a basketball instead.

I have to go now. My volleyball said there was a ship on the horizon. Maybe they got my resume!

Hope to hear from you someday.
Bob

Bad Advice #2, "It might sound like a bad job, but you never know until you try it"

There are some jobs that are just bad. They're never going to be good, no matter how great your attitude is. Learn to recognize them, and don't apply for them.

Bad Job Posting #1:

- Now hiring motivational speakers for an audience of existentialists
- You'll be speaking to a group of Sartre scholars at their annual symposium: "From Nihilism to Nothingness: Why God is Still Dead and So Are You"
- Your Job: Cheer them up

Bad Job Posting #2:

- Now hiring computer programmer for start-up internet company with a great idea and absolutely no practical skills related to IT, programming or coding, assuming they're the same thing – we don't really know, that's why we need you!
- Exciting opportunity to take the lead in explaining everything about computers to us
- We have an awesome idea that nobody's ever thought of before, and we're going to be rich! We just need someone who can translate this idea into a website, mobile app, and all the other variables that are so critical to getting this idea off the ground
- Stock options available, once we get to that point
- It helps if you have some experience in marketing too. And a business plan!

Bad Advice #3, "You have to know when to quit"

You have to learn how to make peace with rejection because you can never give up on something that you truly believe in, including a job or career. When I began my job search, I didn't handle rejection very well. But now, I have no problem with it, because I've had a lot of experience being rejected. In fact, now I look forward to rejection when I wake up in the morning.

I clap my hands, I look in the mirror and I ask myself, "How can I be rejected today?" It's all about pride. Everyone deals with rejection at some point in his or her life. Successful people see it as an opportunity for growth, and make it work to their advantage. Lazy people just stop trying. Rejection management is something that can be mastered, just like anything else, if you're willing to put in the time. If you're interested in learning more about overcoming rejection, a new state of the art rejection clinic was opened last year in Burbank, California. Unfortunately, no one has been accepted into the clinic just yet.

Chapter 4

The Comeback Interview

With the memory of my sweaty encounter with Janet Power in New York still fresh in my mind, I thought it was time to brush up on my interviewing skills. So, I went out and talked to as many people as I could about their recent job-interview experience. I read every book available on the subject, and I participated in over one thousand high-stakes mock interviews. Here's what I learned about the two most commonly used interview formats.

The Traditional Interview

The traditional interview format is still the most widely used method for evaluating job applicants. Wear conservative clothing, but remember to stand out from the crowd with your own unique style. Prepare and memorize thoughtful, detailed responses to anticipated questions, but avoid using pre-prepared answers. Try out your handshake on your friends and family, but don't appear too rehearsed or polished. Ask your parents what their first impression of you was. And think about how you can do better. Create a ten-point strategy for self-improvement. And remember: relax and just be yourself!

Alan of the Comeback

Alan participated in a very unorthodox traditional interview, and he was happy to talk to me about his experience.

"So, Alan, I understand that you were successful in landing the job – congratulations."

"Thank you." Alan smiled.

"So – what was the interview like?" I asked.

"...Actually it didn't go very well."

"Really – how so?"

"Well, about halfway through the interview I was actually arrested."

"...Arrested? Like, by the police?"

"Yes. There was a sting operation, and about fifteen minutes into the interview, the cops burst through the door – five of them – quite unexpectedly, indicating in very strong words that the interview was now over."

"That sounds pretty bad. So, how did you end up getting the job? I mean – that's quite a remarkable comeback."

"You know, you just have to keep your chin up, and put a positive spin on things, especially if you want to work in public relations. When they knocked down the door, at first I thought maybe this organization had a zero tolerance policy towards lying, and so I suspected that they had discovered that I hadn't been completely forthcoming about why I had left my previous employer, but then I realized that wasn't the case, so then I knew that it must have been some kind of a misunderstanding."

"Was it?"

"...Oh yes, it was very much a misunderstanding. It turns out that I have the same name – and quite similar DNA – to a very nasty Colombian drug lord, so when I applied for this position, the HR people suspected that I was in fact this drug lord because of my name and my background in pharmaceuticals. Then, they ran my DNA and they were almost certain."

"How did they run your DNA?"

"That information is available online these days – in fact, there's an app for that now, and most prospective employers will do a DNA screening and fingerprint analysis as part of the interview process."

"That sounds rather invasive..." I had heard about these types of privacy issues related to the job hunt.

"Yes, it is invasive, and of course it's designed to prevent this very thing from happening – so that you're not mistaken for a drug lord. But in this case, the system failed."

"I would agree with that. So, what did you do? How did you go from being arrested to being hired?"

"It's all about a winning attitude; you have to believe in yourself, even when the chips are down. So, once I realized that this was all a huge misunderstanding, I decided to proceed with the interview."

"How did you proceed with the interview when you were being taken away in the back of a squad car?" I asked.

"Well, I couldn't answer any more questions about my background – the conversation was pretty much over at that point – but I could demonstrate confidence, organizational ability, and multitasking skills in the face of a hostile and rather stressful work environment, so that's what I did. I knew that my prospective employer would eventually learn the truth about me – that I was innocent – so I held the upper hand in that regard."

"So, what happened?"

"Well, as I was being led to the backseat of the police car, there was a crowd of people gathering, and they were all saying things like, 'There's no way that guy's getting hired,' but

I just flashed a very confident, winning smile and gave them all a thumbs-up, and then I did the 'victory sign' with my hands – just like Richard Nixon – before I got into the police cruiser."

"That's inspiring."

"Well, body language is absolutely critical – it's much more important than what you're saying or what's happening in terms of external cues – so I was able to manage the meta-narrative and make the best of what appeared to be a losing situation."

"So, how did you end up getting hired?" I asked.

"Two days later, I was released from police custody when a more extensive DNA test was performed. The police department and my prospective employer both officially apologized to me and I was able to reschedule the interview. We just picked up right where we left off, before the sting operation."

"So, what kinds of questions did they ask you, during the second interview?"

"Mainly, they wanted to know if I was going to sue them, and I assured them that I wouldn't do that – I just needed a job, and I had no interest in retribution. I figured – that was all just water under the bridge; these things happen all the time. And so once we got past the awkwardness of my being arrested, we had a very positive discussion about my future."

"So, what kind of work are you doing for them now?"

"I was hired as regional director of their international staffing division – and I love the work. I've increased their client base by over three hundred percent in just two quarters. We're launching a new ad campaign called "Victory" – our target clients are job seekers who have not represented themselves well, either on paper or in person. We reframe their narrative with a preemptive and highly confident body-language blitz that showcases their potential in a game-changing way; we take a disastrous, near-death job application, and we turn it into something magnificent."

"That's wonderful, Alan."

Alan has since been promoted to Vice President of International Media and Public Relations at his company. He is currently working on a book about the vast and unlimited power of body language to reshape our destiny and resurrect our dreams, in the job hunt and beyond.

The Panel Interview

The panel interview differs from the traditional one-on-one interview in that there will usually be at least four interviewers seated across from you at the table. The goal of the panel interview is to ascertain the candidate's ability to operate within the context of a group dynamic, and to effectively address a small audience in a high stakes situation.

Leonard, from Spokane, Washington, took part in a fairly stressful and rather unique panel interview during his job hunt, and he shared his experience with me.

Leonard of the Lion

"Well, I suspected that I was walking into a panel interview, because a friend of mine worked at *RBI58 Associates*, where I was interviewing, and he told me that they normally relied upon this style of interviewing. Also, the position I was interviewing for was going to involve a lot of public speaking, so I'm sure they wanted to get a sense for how I handled that kind of situation. But still, I just wasn't prepared for how seriously they took the whole thing."

"What do you mean?" I asked.

"Well, I walked into what looked like an amphitheater, and there was a crowd of at least eighteen thousand screaming interviewers out there. It was like a coliseum or something, and they had these people way back in the stands that were shouting at me with questions. There was a lot of smoke and incense, and they even had some half-naked guy pounding a conga drum back there. It was just really intense, you know. Like some kind of Aztec sacrifice ritual."

"I probably would've just left."

“Yeah, well anyway, so when I couldn’t answer their question about my experience developing corporate revenue sharing strategies, it was like a riot broke out there. People were getting thrown all over, and there was this deafening roar coming from the crowd, and I just knew I wasn’t getting the job. I saw a lion running around out there in the audience, among the charging bodies and war paint.”

I hadn’t met any lions on my job hunt so far.

Leonard continued. “Yes, it was all very Indiana Jones-like; it was kind of exciting, except that I was really nervous about that lion. He turned out to be a really friendly animal, and his name was ‘Jolly.’ I thought that was nice how they named him ‘Jolly,’ but I don’t know if I’d want to work at a place that keeps a lion, even if he has a friendly-sounding name. The whole thing was very unusual; it was probably the most intense interview experience I’ve ever had. People were shouting and heckling me, and I couldn’t get a word in edgewise. It reminded me of our corporate conference in Atlanta last year, when Bob crashed the server in payroll. All hell broke loose, as you can imagine. People were getting thrown all over, kind of like this interview, but there was no lion in Atlanta."

Leonard did not land the job, but he befriended the lion, and took him home with him after the interview, despite strong protest from his cat "Lulu," a small domestic short-hair. Leonard brings Jolly with him when he gives speeches at corporate conferences around the country, as a freelance motivational speaker. Leonard proudly noted that nobody has heckled him yet, with Jolly in attendance.

Chapter 5

Coping with Rejection

A Conversation with
Dr. Lester P. Lotus, Ph.D.

The psychological dynamics of job-hunting and rejection are unfortunately not properly addressed in most mainstream job-hunting handbooks. Studies indicate that ninety five percent of all job seekers experience significant depression and feelings of hopelessness, rejection and anger at some point in their job search. These feelings are normal and should not be ignored. While they generally subside within two weeks of securing full-time employment, it's helpful to think creatively about how to deal with these feelings during the job hunt, so that they don't overwhelm you and hamper your employment prospects.

For help in dealing with these powerful emotions, I sought out the advice of Dr. Lester P. Lotus, Ph.D. Dr. Lotus is a licensed family therapist and conflict mitigation consultant. He holds a Ph.D. in Anger Resolution, and has an extremely calming demeanor. He was recently cited by *Positive Energy Monthly* as a rising star in the field of interpersonal dynamics and anger management techniques. He is among the top ten most empathetic individuals in the world, and was recently appointed to the president's *National Task Force on Peace and Wellbeing*. He first rose to national attention following an incident in 2014 aboard a bus in Seattle, where he reportedly broke up an armed robbery with a spontaneous group hug. Since the incident in Seattle, Dr. Lotus has been called in as a consultant to develop strategies to reduce crime in twenty of the nation's largest cities. After he moved to Miami the crime rate dropped by nearly fifty percent following the deployment of Lotus's revolutionary new anti-crime tactic known as

"Emergency Love." I sat down with Dr. Lotus in his office in Miami.

"Well, it's difficult, I know, coping with the rejection that you feel during the job search. It can be very scary, and that's okay. I know how difficult it can be, because I've been there too, and people need to know that it's alright to feel this way. We need to get this message out now – that everything's okay."

Dr. Lotus stared at me intently for a moment, and then suddenly stood up and walked over to the window and then shouted loudly into the street: "You are loved! All of you!!"

He returned to his seat, gazed at me for a moment, and then continued. "...So we need to get this message out to people who are still looking for jobs. They need to know that they're not alone, because it can be very disconcerting and very disruptive to the process of self-actualization. It's very healthy to have these feelings, and it's important to talk about those feelings, to share your feelings. It's all part of the healing process." Dr. Lotus had a deeply empathetic look in his eyes, and at several times during our discussion it appeared as if he were either going to embrace me or perhaps run to the window and start shouting about love again. His black turtleneck hugged his neck, and he stroked his goatee while speaking with a gentle and relaxing cadence. It rained softly outside, and Dr. Lotus offered me homemade chocolate chip cookies while pausing to observe a yellow finch on a tree outside his office.

"Thank you," I said. The cookies were extraordinary.

Dr. Lotus continued. "It's just not fair, I know, because you have to be confident and strong to get a job, but when you don't have a job, you don't feel very confident or very strong, and that can be very difficult and very intimidating. So I encourage my patients to talk about that, to work through those emotions." Dr. Lotus showed me a picture of his cat, Fluffy, which he kept on his desk next to his collection of stuffed animals. Dr. Lotus's demeanor became quite intense as he recounted the day it all changed for him.

"...Well, I was in a very negative place in my life, and I had recently been laid off from my previous job as a facilitator for an educational consulting firm. They just didn't need me anymore, and they decided to end the relationship, and it was a very hurtful time in my life. My cat, Fluffy, was ignoring me and giving me nasty looks, as if the whole situation were my fault."

"My cat does that too," I said.

"Yes, cats will do that. It's their way, and we need to accept that and celebrate them for who they are," Dr. Lotus advised me.

Presently Fluffy entered the room and jumped up onto Dr. Lotus's desk. Fluffy stared directly into my eyes with a passive aggressive glare. He didn't seem to be very happy that I was there. He looked exactly like the picture on Dr. Lotus's desk.

Dr. Lotus continued. "I had been unemployed for almost a year, and I had pretty much gotten used to being ignored – it seemed that nobody would respond to any of my applications or inquiries. And one day when I was already feeling very low, my cat gave me this really hurtful look, and then began chewing on my very favorite meditation book, and I just couldn't take it anymore." Fluffy looked off towards the window, pretending not to listen.

"What did you do?" I asked.

"Well, I said to the cat, 'This isn't fair. I don't deserve to be treated this way, and I find this type of behavior very hostile, and I just don't understand why you would eat my meditation books like this. Why are you being so hurtful? Why are you doing this to me?' And I was in tears, and I think the cat was very taken aback, and usually he would just run under the bed when I spoke to him like this."

Fluffy looked like someone who often ran under the bed.

"So, what happened?"

"Well, we actually had a very healthy dialogue that day, and we talked for hours, and it helped me to see things from the cat's perspective. I was crying, and the cat was crying, and we just really cleared the air. It turns out that his needs weren't being met, and I had neglected to take him for walks as frequently as he would have liked, and he wasn't happy with the cat food that I'd been giving him. It was a new generic brand – not locally grown – and it made him feel very sad and underappreciated. And it turns out that he was also very concerned about me, and he felt that there was nothing he could do to help me. I mean, what can a cat do?"

"I'm not sure." I was still thinking about Dr. Lotus walking his cat, wondering how that worked. Did he use a leash or did the cat just follow along?

"…Well, he had tried to bring me a mouse once, but I told him that I didn't want a mouse, and so he felt like a failure. So, I was able to see things from his perspective, and it was a very constructive and positive dialogue that we had. And it helped me to realize that sometimes cats will be very nasty, when they're really just scared inside, and unhappy about themselves. And once I realized that, it gave me a whole new perspective on dealing with nasty cats – and mean people – during my job search, and I think that really helped me."

"How did it help you?" I asked.

"Well, I was able to take those very negative and sad emotions, and turn them into something more life-affirming. And once I did that, I found a new job very easily. And now I'm surrounded by a positive energy, and I'm in a much happier place. And that's very healthy. And I owe that to Fluffy. Thank you, Fluffy."

"What a beautiful story about the bond that exists between a man and a cat," I observed.

Dr. Lotus nodded. He offered me another batch of chocolate chip cookies while explaining that during his job search, he encountered many people who acted out in a way that was similar to Fluffy. He said that his experience with Fluffy gave him the insight he needed to deal with them in a more positive way, to transform their hidden sadness into a happier life energy that helped him get hired.

Dr. Lotus continued sharing. "Well, there was this one gentleman in the Human Resources department of a particular telecommunications firm that will remain nameless, and he said some very hurtful and derogatory things to me when I called him to inquire about a job that I had applied to several weeks earlier."

"I've heard many derogatory things during my job search as well."

"Yes, well we all know what that's like," Dr. Lotus frowned and began speaking in a slightly more hushed tone. "It was really quite shocking. I simply asked him if they had received my resume, and he mocked me and told me that I should never have applied for the job because I wasn't qualified and I was wasting his time. He began using some very hurtful and pejorative language, and I found it very unprofessional and mean-spirited."

"How did you handle it?"

"Well, I was about to end the conversation right there, when I realized that I was dealing with Fluffy all over again. It was the same emotional dynamic, and I could really tell that this man was hurting inside. If he were a cat, there's no doubt in my mind that he would have been chewing up my collection of meditation books at that very moment."

"I've met a lot of people like that." There was a powerful appetite out there for meditation books.

Dr. Lotus nodded. "And people aren't mean to strangers unless they have some hidden pain, and it was clear that this man had a lot of hurt inside, so I confronted him about it. I told him that he was making me very sad, and I asked him why he was being so hurtful. And he was silent for a minute or two, and then he started shouting at me about the money he'd lost on the NASDAQ. But when he was all done shouting at me, he was quiet for a minute, and I just listened – allowing him space to just be as he was – without judgment or emotional reactivity. And within a few minutes he began talking quite despondently about how miserable his job was, and how he just couldn't understand why anyone would actually be applying for a job with his company. He told me that his job was like a 'slow death interrupted by an occasional staff meeting and a soggy bagel.'"

"I've heard that many jobs are like that." I was beginning to feel compassion for the man that Dr. Lotus was telling me about.

Dr. Lotus continued. "So I told him that it was very healthy to grieve in this way, and I urged him to leave his job. It was a very positive phone conversation for me, because I realized that this was in fact not the right place for me to work. And I would never have known that had I not vigorously confronted his aggression with my own compassion." Dr. Lotus interrupted our conversation to check on a new batch of chocolate chip cookies that were being prepared in the kitchen adjacent to his office. The soothing smells of rising cookie dough and melted chocolate wafted through the hallway. Dr. Lotus returned with a fresh batch. Fluffy was interested in the cookies, but pretended not to be.

Dr. Lotus spoke more quietly now. "There was another incident, during an interview I had for a position as a human resources facilitator with an inventory consulting firm, and I found myself under attack by some very unhappy people. I had just come back for the second interview, and while I was sitting down to prepare for the interview, this very angry man walked in and began firing all these very hurtful and pointed questions at me, asking me to explain why I had left my previous job. I guess he didn't like my explanation about why my previous employer had decided to end the relationship, and he just kept at me during the whole interview."

"Why was he being so rude?"

"Well, he was a very unhappy man, and I think my inner contentedness threatened him. He had a very accusing tone, and he was absolutely fixated on the question of why I had left the previous company. Then he started interrogating me about my spreadsheet skills, and he told me that it would be very unusual for them to hire someone who had so little experience working with *Microsoft Excel*, and he was just being very provocative, trying to make me feel inadequate about spreadsheets."

"They can be very challenging."

"And then he launched into this diatribe about how I was completely unqualified for the position because I had never given a *TED* talk in my entire life, and he told me that he was one of the best *TED* talkers in the entire office. It was very hurtful. He just made me feel very unqualified."

"Don't feel bad," I reassured Dr. Lotus. "I've actually never given a *TED* talk either, and I'm terrible with spreadsheets. I've never been very good with the advanced functions, like macros and pivot tables."

Dr. Lotus looked at me with an appreciative expression. "...And then the other man started glaring at my resume while I sat there silently, and he began rolling his eyes as he read through it, and I really thought he was about to shred it right there in front of me."

"...Like, with a paper shredder?"

"Oh yes – I've seen it done before."

"That seems kind of harsh."

"It is harsh, and I was worried that it might happen to my resume on this particular day, so before I let that happen, I just stood up, and I did what I always do when things get out of hand. I gave them a big group-hug, continental style."

"What's a continental style hug?" I asked.

"It's where you lift the person off the ground with the force of your embrace."

"Okay."

"So, they were speechless, and we hugged for at least a minute or two, and then I sat down, and their eyes were extremely wide and they looked very frightened, and I could tell that they were very confused. I told them that everything was going to be okay, and then I offered them some chocolate chip cookies that I had brought along with me in my satchel. And the man that looked like he was going to shred my resume, well he just got up and ran away."

"That was nice of you – to offer them cookies." It had never occurred to me to bring a satchel full of cookies to a job interview.

"…And the other man, the one who had made me feel inadequate because I had never given a *TED* talk, well he just sat there. He really didn't know what to say. I would guess that about five minutes passed while we just sat in each other's presence, saying nothing. It was beautiful. And then finally after the long silence, he started speaking excitedly in Italian, and then he stood up and gave me this enormous bear hug. He was trembling with joy, and he was telling me in Italian that he actually hated giving *TED* talks, and that he really wanted to be an opera singer. And then he started belting out a line from Puccini's *La Boheme*, and the window nearly shattered because he sang so loud, and it turns out that he had the most beautiful voice." Dr. Lotus rushed to his stereo, and we were soon overwhelmed by the lush sounds of Pavarotti lamenting the death of *Mimi*. Fluffy purred loudly as the richly textured sonorities flooded into the room. It was obvious that Fluffy was familiar with this particular aria.

Lotus became excited and began speaking very loudly, projecting his voice over the sounds of Pavarotti. “So I congratulated him on his voice, and told him that he should be very proud of his gift, and he confided in me that he was going to leave his job in two weeks, and audition for the role of *Rodolfo* in an off-Broadway production next spring. I told him that it was very brave for him to share that with me, and then we both started singing, in Italian. It was marvelous! It was a spontaneous celebration of life and all things positive!”

“That’s a beautiful story,” I yelled over the music.

Lotus continued shouting enthusiastically. “Yes, well, I’m actually quite an avid opera fan, and I find that the music really helps me while I’m meditating in the evenings, and it just exudes the most poignant life energy, and it makes me feel in harmony with all living creatures. So we were both singing these Italian librettos very loudly, with tears in our eyes, and other people in the office started gathering around us, and they were staring in disbelief. And then it was a miracle, because some of the other employees started joining in. The office manager turned out to be the most amazing soprano, and she started singing the lines of *Mimi* right there near the water cooler, and before you know it, some of the interns joined in with their own rendition of *Che gelida manina!* It was just a beautiful moment, and we were all in tears. After the singing, we all had a group hug. Some of those people have become my dearest of friends – there is so much love!"

At this point, Dr. Lotus's eyes were tearing up and he was waving his handkerchief through the air in imitation of *Rodolfo*. He ran to the window and proclaimed to the world once more: "You are loved!! All of you!"

"So, did you get the job?" I shouted.

"No, but it turned out to be a blessing nonetheless. As it happened, twelve of the employees at this particular inventory consulting firm quit their jobs that day to become actors, and they helped me find my next job as a creative therapist for the *Broadway Actors Guild!* And I loved this job very much, and it was very good to me. I met some of the most beautiful and warmest people in the world, and we had many wonderful and intimate moments together, and we cried a lot, and we were very happy to be together in such a positive, life-affirming work environment. And all of this, I owe to Fluffy." Lotus began singing an aria in honor of Fluffy. I couldn't help but join in.

At the end of our discussion, Dr. Lotus, Fluffy, and I were all belting out the aria from Act Three of Puccini's Madama Butterfly. We ended our meeting with a group hug, and a tearful, heartfelt goodbye. Dr. Lotus took down my address, and assured me that he would send me a batch of chocolate chip cookies during the Holidays each year. He also invited me back to Miami to attend Fluffy's birthday party next month.

Chapter 6

Career Changing Currents

I was inspired by Dr. Lotus's story. I envied the relationship that he had with his cat, but I knew that Fluffy was a special creature, and so it was perhaps unrealistic to expect that every cat would be there for their owner during the darkest hour of their job hunt, and fearlessly stand by them as they embarked on a new career path. So, I wondered – how did people change careers on their own? Without a Fluffy in their life? And more broadly, what led people to make that change? What specifically did they not like about the jobs that they had before? What was their strategy? What were they looking for? Were they successful? Was it even possible to change careers in this economy? Why / why not?

Jennifer of the Stage

Jennifer used to work as a fuel analyst with a large U.S. – based petroleum company before quitting her job to pursue her dreams of becoming a Broadway actor. I spoke with Jennifer in her apartment in Brooklyn.

"I was making a comfortable living as a fuels analyst, but I knew there was something missing, I just didn't know what it was. I was out walking my dog one night last June, and I looked up at the stars, and I remembered when I was a kid, and how I used to look up at the stars at night, and I would dream about becoming an actor. I never dreamt about gasoline."

"So how did you get into the fuel business?" I asked.

"Well, that's just where I ended up. I don't know how it happened, but I didn't get into law school, and I never seriously considered the whole acting thing. I needed a 'real job.' So they had an opening at this oil company, and my friend from college knew a guy who worked in the sales division, so next thing you know I'm a fuels analyst, and I did that for eight years."

"What was that like?" I only had a casual knowledge of fuel.

"I made a good living, and I can tell you all about the cracking and refinement process, and I can talk about every nuance related to hydrocarbons and the petroleum commodities index at the Chicago Mercantile Exchange. I know everything there is to know about butane spheres and how Alaskan downstream crude capacity affects the *BCD* rates at these refineries in the northeast, but I can't say that I ever loved the stuff. There was something missing. No magic, you know."

"I can see that." I barely enjoyed filling up the gas tank in my car.

Jennifer nodded in agreement before continuing. "They say you can teach someone to become a good fuels analyst, but a *great* fuels analyst is just born. You either have it, or you don't. And I knew I'd never be one of the great ones. Not like Kminsky or Delario. These guys were just *legends* in the fuel world. I once heard that Kminsky invented a whole new language for himself based on the Chicago Mercantile Exchange *BCD* ratios. Only three people on the planet could understand him. They say he once recited the entire *OPEC 2014 Annual Crude Earnings Report* from memory – in the original dialect!"

"That's brilliant."

"It's awesome! You know what I'd give to be able to do that? I couldn't even recite the first page! Kminsky was one of those rare gems who had fuel in his blood. It was like Alaskan crude just ran through his veins. There was no stopping him on the floor of the Chicago Mercantile Exchange. The guy was almost flammable – a true legend. I knew I would never be *that good*. I just never fell in love with gasoline."

"So how did you know it was time to leave? When did you decide to become an actor?" I asked.

"...Well, it wasn't like I had a big revelation and everything suddenly changed overnight – it was more of a gradual building of dissatisfaction with my job, to the point where I just couldn't do it anymore. Turning thirty was part of it, I think – I started asking myself if I really wanted to spend the rest of my life doing something that I didn't feel any passion towards. So I walked away from fuel – I quit my job a year ago."

"That's great – and how's it going now?"

"Well, to be honest, not so well. It's a tough transition. I couldn't even get a job waiting tables, so I started doing temp work, and that's been pretty rough, actually. I answer phones for a pharmaceutical company when I'm not filing documents for a state agency. It's really boring."

“And how are the auditions going?” I asked.

“Brutal. You’ve got five hundred people lined up outside the door before five AM, but nobody gets a chance to be heard because we’re not part of the actors’ union. I’m not sure what I was thinking when I quit my fuel job. I didn’t realize how hard it would be. I’m running out of savings and pretty soon I won’t be able to afford living on a temp’s salary.”

“Well, at least you’re being true to yourself – following your dreams.”

“Yeah, I’m not sure about that either – working as a temp definitely gives me more flexibility to go to auditions, but you know – people should be more honest when they tell you to just follow your dreams, unless you’ve got a huge amount of money in savings. It’s not all Joseph Campbell or *The Alchemist* – sometimes following your bliss doesn’t pan out for everyone. There’s a reason people stay in jobs they don’t totally love.”

“I hate thinking that way. It’s very depressing.”

“Me too, but that’s the way of the world. We can’t all get paid to do what we love.” Jennifer let out a sigh and threw a chew toy towards her dog, Roller, who lunged at the toy in a wagging manner. Roller appeared to love his job.

"Well, maybe give it some more time."

"Yeah, maybe, but I'll probably go back to fuel someday. The pay was good, I didn't mind the work, and the job didn't beat me down like these jobs do, so maybe it'll give me more time to do the acting thing on the side – you know, after work – after fuel."

"Well, best of luck to you."

After two more heroic years in New York, Jennifer eventually got a job as a waitress and finally landed a supporting role in a popular commercial for dental floss. Unfortunately, the commercial didn't lead to any other commercials, and she has since returned to her former field of fuel analysis. However, she will be co-starring in a local production of an avant-garde play exploring investment diversification strategies in the afterlife. She told me that while she was very happy with her new life, she was not entirely happy with the new play.

John of the Degrees

John is a nice guy trying to change careers. He works as a computer systems analyst, but he would like to become a high school English teacher. He's affable, articulate, and appears to have a very high level of emotional intelligence.

"So John, you're looking to change careers, is that right?"

"Yes. I've been working as a systems analyst for twenty years now, and that's been great – the pay is fantastic – but I really want something with a more human touch. I've watched my own boys as they struggle with high school, and I see how important it is to have good teachers, and I think I could make a difference – I think I could be an awesome teacher, and I really want to try that."

"Why now? Why leave a lucrative career that you're good at?"

"I just turned fifty, and I took stock of my life, and I realized that I didn't want to work in computers forever. My wife suggested teaching because I really enjoy learning new things, and I'm always talking with a lot of nostalgia about high school and some of the great teachers that I had, and the more I thought about it, the more I realized that this would be a good move for me. In fact, my wife is a teacher, and she loves it, and she's always thought that I'd make a fantastic teacher."

"Great. So, how's it going? Has it been a smooth transition?"

"Not really, no. It turns out that it's very difficult to start a new career. It seems that when it comes to finding a job in education, experience is all that matters."

"But it sounds like you'd make a great teacher."

"Yes – I think I would, but I probably won't have the opportunity to demonstrate that because I've never taught before. People don't tell you this, but the first job you take out of college is absolutely critical because it creates a kind of momentum that builds over time. Once you get experience in a particular field, it's very difficult to make the transition into a new field – it's like there's this career track inertia that keeps you from stepping outside the box. The job market pegs you into one field, and it's very difficult to break out of that mold."

"But couldn't you get some experience? Maybe do some substitute teaching?"

"Yeah – I've been trying to do that, but so far nothing has panned out – HR people have actually told me that I'm over-qualified and too old to be a substitute teacher, and it's frustrating because I'm not qualified enough to have my own classroom. But of course the only way to get that experience is by substitute teaching, which nobody will hire me to do right now."

"That would be frustrating."

"Yes – and it's not enough to have experience – many schools won't even look at your resume unless you have a master's degree in education, and of course I don't have that." John sighed.

"But we need smart, passionate people to go into teaching – I don't know why the schools would make that so difficult."

"I've been struggling with that one for months now, and I have a theory."

"What's your theory?" I asked.

"Well, I have several friends who have also tried shifting careers, and their experiences have been very similar to my own. I've noticed that our economy is not very fluid – we place undue emphasis on experience and degrees while often ignoring the larger question of whether a job candidate would actually be good at doing that particular job."

"Why do you think we do that?"

"Well, of course there are some highly skilled careers that do require degrees and experience: surgeons, pilots, air-traffic controllers, paramedics, engineers, etc., but there are so many careers that fall into that gray area where you might not really need a degree or experience to be good in that field: teaching, writing, acting, management, human resources, advertising, social work, sales, etc., but here's the thing – we all want to believe that our particular field is really demanding and that it requires a high level of skill; that enhances our ego and it reflects well on our accomplishments, so we create these artificially high barriers to enter our chosen career, and we resent it when new people want to do our jobs without paying homage to how complicated and difficult our work is. The irony is that the social significance of our work is not a function of how complicated or difficult it is; actors don't need experience or master's degrees to do a great job, and yet, what they do is so important for society – they show us our humanity. Who cares whether they have a degree or not? And I think the same is true for so many other professions."

"So you think that we make it difficult for people to change careers because some people's egos are too heavily invested in their own careers?"

"Well, not consciously – but yes, I think that's definitely a factor in why our job market is not more fluid. I mean, we have all these master's degrees in fields that don't really require degrees, and nowadays everybody's getting a PhD in something – partly so they can feel more important. But the result is that we're making it harder for really great people to enter new careers that they might be really good at – we're calcifying our economy with all these bogus requirements."

"I think you might be onto something there. I've always wondered why so many principals and school superintendents need to have a master's or PhD in education, for example."

"Exactly – what does that even mean? It's not the same as biology or quantum physics, but we pretend that it is because we think that it gives education more gravitas – and everybody seems to want a little gravitas – but of course things don't need to be complicated to be important. But we all go along with the charade. The problem is that the charade is hurting us; if we require a master's degree for someone to be a principal, then we're preventing some really great people from running our schools. They might have it in them to do a fantastic job, but they'll never get the chance because they don't have the right degree. It's kind of insane."

"Well, I hope you get the chance to become a teacher."

"I hope so too. Thanks."

John put his dream of becoming a teacher on hold a few months after we spoke. With his two boys about to go to college, he couldn't afford to pursue a master's degree in education right now, and nobody wanted to hire him without any prior teaching experience. John has since begun volunteering as a language tutor for non-English speakers at the local community center, and he very much enjoys the work. So far, none of his students have asked him what his teaching qualifications are.

Carol of the Bored

Carol is not a happy person. She is stuck in a job that she doesn't like and, according to Carol, her colleagues are incompetent, boring and heavy. She is too smart and dynamic for her job, which she views as a mistake that she hasn't yet recovered from. She doesn't like me, and she probably doesn't like you either. I spoke with Carol from her office, which was decorated in drab colors and negative energy.

"Thanks for agreeing to talk with me."

"That's fine. So, you're writing a book about job-hunting?" Carol almost looked curious, but not quite. 'Curious' was too strong a word to describe her demeanor.

"Yes – it's an assortment of different conversations I've had with fictional characters about job-hunting, and I was hoping to include my conversation with you in the chapter about changing careers."

"I'd rather that you didn't call me a fictional character."

"Sorry – what would you like me to call you?"

"I don't know, just call me Carol. Anyway, let's get on with it. I've got a lot of work to do."

"Right, so I understand that you're not all that happy with your job?"

"No, I'm not." Carol lit a cigarette. "...But it's a job, so it's not supposed to be fun, and I understand that, but it's boring as hell." She puffed smoke in the face of a red and yellow Cubist self-portrait of herself frowning on the wall above her desk.

“Have you thought about leaving?” I asked.

“Everyday – I never wanted to do this – it was just something I fell into because I needed a job.” Carol began to grimace from a lower back pain, which she told me about in extensive detail for the next ten minutes. I learned a lot about sciatica, but I’m not going to include that part of the conversation here.

“What kind of work do you do, exactly?” I asked.

“…You know, I’ve never really been sure of my exact job title, but I work with resource management controls and technology interface solutions – which is a lot like data acquisition.”

I wasn’t interested in finding out what that meant, so I steered the conversation towards something else. “So, what would your ideal job be like, if you weren’t doing this?”

“My ideal job would be getting paid to do nothing, and not being surrounded by idiots.” Carol puffed smoke in my face now.

"I see – so, your colleagues are difficult?"

"They're not difficult – they're stupid." She inhaled the smoke.

"So, I guess you don't hang out with them much at lunch?" I asked.

"Why would I do that? I don't have time for lunch." Carol snarled at me.

"Is there anything that you like about the job?"

"I like Fridays, but sometimes I get annoyed because it means there's only two more days until Monday, and I absolutely hate Mondays. I don't like Tuesdays either, because they feel like Mondays. Wednesdays are just bland, but I suppose that Thursdays are alright, when they don't drag on forever. But Monday totally kills my weekend – just knowing that it's coming – that really puts a damper on my Sundays, but Saturdays are okay, except that I'm usually too tired to enjoy them."

I could feel the positive energy being drained from my body as Carol invited me into her bleak, smoky worldview where everything was annoying and stupid.

"Carol, I wouldn't normally say this to a non-fictional person, but your attitude is awful."

"…Why should I care?" Carol asked me pointedly. Her face was barely visible now, through the dense fog of nicotine.

"I guess there's no reason to care. But it's just depressing."

"Who cares? I'm a fictional character - remember? I can be whoever I want to be. Besides – what am I doing in your chapter about changing careers? There's no way that's going to happen. The economy is total crap, and I'm going nowhere."

"Well, it's not a foregone conclusion that you have to stay in this job that you hate. I mean, isn't that up to you?"

"It's not up to me – it's up to you. I'm just a shadow of your imagination, remember?" The Cubist self-portrait of Carol seemed to smirk at me through the fog.

"Well, this isn't how I imagined you."

"And you're not so great yourself."

"Fair enough, but suppose that you could find a different career – a different life – would you want that?"

"Of course I'd want that, but how is that going to happen?"

"Well, what if I could write it that way?"

"Then do it – just rewrite this whole goddamned chapter. Get me out of this crap job."

"Okay, so how should I rewrite it? What kind of job would you like?"

"I told you I wanted a job where I got paid for doing nothing and I wasn't surrounded by idiots – that's all I ask."

"That's really what you want?"

"That's exactly what I want." Carol almost smiled, but not exactly. 'Smile' was too strong a word to describe Carol's face.

So I rewrote this chapter a little bit here, obviously. Carol is no longer working in resource management controls and technology interface solutions. She is now working from home in her new full-time position that doesn't require anything at all. She receives a paycheck every two weeks via direct deposit and her salary gives her plenty of money to spend, as she sees fit. Her employer provides health insurance. She orders groceries online and her lifestyle doesn't require any contact with the idiots of the outside world. Her only human contact is with her cat, Mr. Truffles, who is rude, and not really a human. I visited Carol in her home exactly one year after I rewrote her job to her specifications.

"So Carol, how are things going with the new job?"

"Things are fine with the job – it's pretty easy, since they require nothing, but my back still aches and my cat has turned into a complete jerk since I stopped leaving the house."

Mr. Truffles kind of looked like a jerk, so I wasn't completely surprised to hear this. He had tried to bite me when I entered the house.

"Well, at least you have your life back," I pointed out. "I mean, you don't need to spend all those empty hours in the office doing resource management controls anymore. That must be nice."

"Well, sure, that was nice for a few months, but then it got old, sitting here doing nothing, taking crap from my cat. I watch TV, but there's nothing on. They're all idiots. So, I'm not sure my life is any better since you rewrote my job. It's just the same old stuff, except now I'm at home instead of the office, and the idiots are on TV instead of in person."

"I'm sorry to hear that, Carol. You know, there's no reason you need to stay here at home with your cat. You have plenty of money now, and lots of free time, so why don't you travel? Get out there and meet some nice people? Have some fun."

"Well, that all sounds fine, but my back hurts, and I've already been to Europe, and it wasn't so great. Do you know how expensive it is? And people in France are rude."

"So take up a hobby. Take dance classes or learn a musical instrument."

"Now, why would I do that?" Carol lit another cigarette.

"I don't know, because it's fun?"

"It might be fun to you, but it's not fun to me. And my back hurts."

"Carol, I think you might be depressed."

"I'm not depressed."

"You are definitely depressed. You're full of negativity."

"I told you that I'm not depressed. Besides, even if I were depressed, what would you do about it? Would you just rewrite my personality? Wave your magic wand, and change my life again? You already did that once, and it didn't help me very much, so I'd rather that you just left me alone this time. I don't want you to turn me into somebody I'm not."

"Okay, I'll respect your wishes. But you should know that you're missing out on so many good things, which is a shame. But if you change your mind, and decide that you do want me to rewrite your mood, just let me know, and I can give you a whole new personality – I can literally make you happy. Are you sure you don't want that?"

"I don't want you to change my personality. That's who I am, and I don't want you to take that away from me." The thick fog of nicotine was back.

"Well, it's not really who you are. You're a reflection of my imagination, remember? And I can imagine a much happier version of you, but I don't want to impose that on you if you don't want that, so I'll just wait until you ask me, okay?"

"Yes. That's fine. Now, I need to feed the cat, so if we're all done here, would you please excuse me?"

"Okay, Carol, but you know where to find me."

"Goodbye."

And with that, Carol slammed the door in my face. I turned away from her house, took a deep breath of the cold, clear, smoke-free air, and then went home.

I never heard from Carol, although I did hear from Mr. Truffles, who requested that I rewrite him into a Tibetan Terrier appearing in a completely different part of this book, which I did. His only request was that his new home chapter didn't include any reference to Carol and her dense fog of negativity.

Chapter 7

Entrepreneurial Spirits

An Island, a Confident Man and a Big Yellow Lab

After my desolate conversation with Carol, I was badly in need of some inspiration and positive energy. I also began to wonder if perhaps there was another way of making a living outside of the traditional office job format. I wanted to learn more about the entrepreneurial spirit – what drove people to strike out on their own? How did they do it? What personality traits did they have? Could anyone learn those traits?

I had heard about a famous self-help expert who had transformed his own struggling accounting firm into an enormously successful low-carb self-help theme park complete with hot coal seminars, non-elective parasailing-based personality assessments and a controversial flammable javelin throwing immersion therapy. His name is Tom Brickman, and he is a larger-than-life figure who towers over the world of celebrity empowerment gurus. Widely considered to be the world's most extroverted human being, he is an expert practitioner of both acupuncture and *Kuntao* martial arts, often simultaneously. He has revolutionized the art of business handshakes with his patented *Jun Tao* closed palm grip, which experts predict will soon outpace the traditional open-faced western grip as the world's most popular style of handshaking.

I sent him an email describing the book that I was writing, and asked for a meeting. I found a rather dubious discount airline and flew aboard a vintage flying boat to his private island just west of the Pacific Island chain of Samoa, near the Apolima Atolls. He seemed genuinely delighted to meet me, and after picking me up at the airport in his new modified yellow macrobiotic-powered Hummer, he insisted that I attend the island's Biannual Shrimp Gumbo Festival, which was being held in a wooden hut adjacent to the island's main hotel. The hut was decorated in a mid-nineteenth century nautical Art Deco fusion style, with an imported Caribbean styled tapestry overlaying the walls, a reference to the island's highly intricate and rather dangerous coral reef surroundings.

We sipped a Papaya juice extract at a bamboo-sheathed table with a direct view of the Sala'ilua Volcano on the western shore, while feasting on a plate of smoked haddock and steamed Pacific flounder. The smells of jasmine and eucalyptus wafted into the hut from the dense rainforest surrounding the hotel. Tropical Cockatiel and Kookaburra birds could be heard singing from inside the dark forest canopy. Brickman's enormous Yellow Lab, Buster, rested lazily in a hammock in his own private villa just across from the swimming pool, while a gentle early evening breeze ushered in the salty air of the tropical waters. Buster eyed my dinner plate with keen attention from across the pool. Brickman sported a deep tan, and grinned broadly while flirting with our voluptuous native server in a Samoan dialect. He turned to me with a big smile, and offered a toast in Latin to the Greek God Dionysus, before vigorously attacking his bowl of kiwi pudding.

"Look, I'm having one hell of a good time out here in the South Pacific," Brickman declared. "I got here last month, and spent the first few weeks starting up my own scuba diving business, just for the hell of it. It's a good way to get a feel for the island, and it's always fun meeting the tourists coming in from all over the world. I bought the island a year ago, but this is the first time I actually visited the damned place."

Brickman casually eyed our waitress while sipping his Papaya juice. He smiled, and then took a moment to breathe in the air before continuing.

"I was going through a dry spell last year, looking for my next project, and I happened to stumble upon an episode of 'Hawaii Five-O' one night while I was meditating, and it got me all excited about the ocean, and next thing you know I've got myself a damned island and a scuba company. And now I'm just tickled to death that I went ahead with it. Good way to lighten the spirits, you know." Brickman excused himself to take a moment to sign a few autographs of his new book on naked bond trading, which was quite popular among the island's residents, many of whom were dressed in island-casual business suits made of flowing silk and layered seersucker.

While Brickman was unapologetically brash, I found it difficult not to like him; he had an aura about him that was rather electromagnetic in a fun-loving, narcissistic kind of way.

"So, last week, I met with the prime minister of the island to hash out some ideas I had for developing the local agribusiness economy, which has been slipping quite a bit since the devaluation of the Tala back in 2015. Showed him some ideas I had for letting the currency float off the adjustable peg, to avoid the kind of deflationary pressures we saw last quarter. He's a good guy, and was pretty excited about what I had to say, so we've lined up a few more meetings tomorrow night over at the planetarium club – should be a good time. I'm just doing my part to help the good folks of the island." Brickman leaned back in his chair and surveyed the coastline.

As the sun set over the volcano, our waitress brought us another round of Mango Lime Sangria and a devilish looking Triple-Layered Mocha Almond Torte. A Calypso band in the hut across from the restaurant struck up an island rendition of "Ave Maria," and our conversation naturally moved in the direction of corporate job dissatisfaction.

"…Look, I know it's a damned shame how many people hate their jobs. I know about this, because I hated my job once too. Your job is a big part of your life, and you have to enjoy it. I'll tell you what, before I struck out on my own, I was in this total dead end job with an accounting firm up in Boston, and I was sitting there one day and the guy on the radio said: '*WKRD 93.5* – we make your workday go by faster.' That's when I realized I was just counting down the hours of my life. In my head I heard the guy say: 'we make your *life* go by faster.' So, I just got up and left. Just dumped my shit in the recycling bin and never looked back. I didn't have anything lined up, but I sure as hell knew what I was walking away from, and I knew that path only led to a quick death." Brickman sipped his *Sangria* while his dog ominously eyed my Triple-Layered Mocha Almond Torte.

"Weren't you worried about money? About finding another job?" I asked.

"Hell yeah, I was scared to death. But I was more scared of that goddamned cubicle with the radio station counting down the hours of my life. But I know what you mean. Hey, it's not easy, but there's no excuse for staying in a job you hate. Look, people will tell you, in this economy, you gotta' take what you can get, and most people don't like working anyway, so you might as well just get used to it. Everybody hates working. If you quit your job you'll never find another one. And I think that's a ten ton stack of horse shit."

"How do you know? Have you ever been unemployed for a long time?" I wondered if Brickman had ever experienced moments of self-doubt.

"Hey, I just know. Look man, the whole problem with this unemployment business, it's totally passive. It assumes that there's a job out *there* for you, and you need to go out and find *someone else* to give you that job before you can do it. Well, to hell with that. If you've been looking for work for more than six months, it's time to find a new approach. Don't just think outside the box – get out there and beat the crap out of that damned box. Mess it up, man." Brickman clenched his fist and bit down hard on a cashew.

He jabbed his finger towards my face and continued while pointing at me. "Hey, when you were a kid and your parents gave you a job to do around the house, that didn't mean that there weren't *other* jobs to do, right?"

"Sure." This was true.

"Damned straight! Did you always just wait on your ass for them to *give you* a job before you did some work around the house? There's a ton of crap to do around the house, and the jobs never end if your house is anything like mine. So, I'm just saying, don't wait for someone to tell you what to do – just go out and do it. And if the house doesn't need fixing, then go out and build your own damned house. Start up your own business. That's what I did, and it was a crap-load of fun. Don't wait for someone to hand you a rake or a paint brush; get out there and see what needs to be done, and then do it yourself."

"Yeah, but you need a lot of cash to start up your own business. Not everyone can do that." I was trying to be realistic.

"Bullshit. Just make it up as you go along, and the money will follow. Don't sit on your ass. It's in you, man. It's in your heart, and it's all under your control. Realizing that is the first step to owning your life. It's about taking control of your own destiny, and not letting the decisions about your future rest in the hands of some human resource drone in an office on the other side of the country. Wake up and dance! Set your own sails, and go for it. It's the island solution." Brickman paused for a moment to gaze at a cruise ship making its way out to sea on the horizon.

I was intrigued by this Brickman guy.

He made some kind of note to himself on his holographic smartphone-like day-planner before continuing. “Look, the only thing that separates the kick ass entrepreneur from the guy punching the time clock every day, is that the entrepreneur believed in his own idea, and he was ready to work his ass off to get there. Whatever it takes man, you just gotta’ do it. It all comes down to old-fashioned hard work, a big idea kind of attitude, and about three tons of rock solid stubbornness. We’ve got a crap load of businesses out there, and someone had to start each and every one of them.”

He took off his sunglasses, and looked me directly in the eyes. “Those folks are just like you and me – just people with a good idea, and a bad ass work ethic. That’s all it ever is: a shitload of hard work. And if you really believe in something, then go for it, man. You just gotta’ find your passion, and work your ass off like you’ve never worked before in your life. And I don’t know about you, but I don’t feel a lot of passion for something like database platform integration – that place you interviewed for back in New York. I mean, what the hell is that? Big mistake. Zero passion.

Nobody wants to be there and nobody should. Somebody needs to stand up and say this is a God Awful waste of time." Brickman flicked a cashew towards the pool. His dog intercepted it in midair.

"Well, some people don't have a choice." Again, I was trying to interject some reason into this conversation.

"Bullshit. You always have choices. Look, I'll tell you a story about my dog, Buster. A couple years ago, that dog was outsourced for a few months because he wasn't pulling his weight around the house." Buster perked up when he heard Brickman talking about him. He listened intently.

"I'll tell you what – I hired that dog with the understanding that he would help me out with the alligator problem I was having on my golf course, but he never liked to chase the damned things – always giving me some lame-ass excuse: 'I'm tired. I'm hungry. The alligators are mean.' Whatever…he was just getting lazy, so I let him go. He really didn't want to be there and it showed." Buster snorted at that remark.

Brickman ignored his dog. “So I brought in this sleek new Tibetan Terrier from Jacksonville – a ferocious little bastard – bred specifically to go after big sport gators and crocs, and he performed beautifully for a couple months, chasing all those gators off the yard, never once complaining when he nearly got bitten in half every morning – tough son of a bitch that terrier was. You should have seen that little dog put a whooping on those gators. Never knew a terrier could be so damned furious.” Brickman leaned back in his chair and motioned for the waitress to bring him a beer.

“And then one night, my old dog Buster comes home unannounced and throws down the gauntlet on that Tibetan Terrier – opens up shop across the street from my house. The old boy started up his own discount gator-hunting business, and built a goddamned doghouse half the size of my own house overlooking the golf course. Made a killing on that gator-hunting business of his, and made the terrier look like a total ass.” Buster rested easily in the hammock while eyeing me with a combative glare.

"So, one day, Buster barges into my house and shows me this absolutely brilliant presentation about why I should hire him back as the top dog of the house, but this time as an equal partner with me. No kidding. He convinced me it was all about ownership, having some stake in the success of the household. He said he'd gotten lazy back when he felt like he was just borrowing the sofa and the doghouse out back. So, he suggested this whole new business model where he would be a live-in houseguest, with the understanding that he would fend for himself, and I wouldn't tell him what to do anymore. Brilliant dog." Buster growled at me while Brickman looked on with amusement. "So, as I sat there listening to Buster give this beautiful presentation, I realized how much the job meant to him, and I saw that he had the passion again, the fire in his eyes – like he was ready to eat some gators. He was making his stand, and laying down the law, and I had to admire the dog. He's a player. The thing about Buster is, he speaks my language, and that's why we get along so well. That dog's a great businessman."

"So, what happened to the terrier?" I asked.

"I fired him. He took some job with a telemarketing outfit overseas. I think he misses chasing gators, but that's life." Buster barked at the mention of the terrier.

"So, I gave Buster his old job back, and promoted him to vice president of sales. And it works great now, because Buster's all over those gators – he can't get enough of them – and he takes a lot of pride in the backyard because he's got a fifty-percent stake in all the profits that we generate on yard sales. He's really doing excellent work these days. It's all about incentives, and having a sense of ownership. It all comes down to pride."

Brickman took a swig from a pint of beer before continuing. "We've got a real free market system going in the kitchen too: if you grab it first, it's yours. We've had ourselves some good fights over dinner, and the dog wins most of them because he's so damned quick with that nose of his, it's like he knows exactly where I keep all the food. He's also got one hell of a left jab, and he's not afraid of using it when he really wants something you've got. So I've been losing weight, but that's the way it goes in the free market – the price of freedom.

God help the pizza delivery guy when he shows up on Friday nights when we order in, because we just land on the bastard."

Brickman grinned at Buster, who continued to eye my Triple-Layered Mocha Almond Torte with an intensely confident gaze. "My dog's a mean son of a bitch, and I'm never going to fire him ever again, because he's earned his position around the house, and he's an equal partner now. He's got the passion, and that's what I'm looking for. That's what everyone's looking for. You can teach an old dog new tricks, but you can't teach him the passion. You either have it, or you don't. And if you don't, then get the hell out of my house."

Buster suddenly jumped from his hammock, and in one graceful motion grabbed my Triple-Layered Mocha Almond Torte in his teeth while flashing an evil dog grin in my face as he flew by. He ran off into the Tiki Lounge with the torte in his mouth. Brickman laughed heartily while clapping and cheering the dog on, beaming with pride.

"...See, Buster understands the rules of the game," Brickman declared with a grin. "If you want something, you go for it. And you go for it with passion, no hesitation. You don't wait around for it to come to you, or else it won't. Just take it, and ask questions later. But you plan the hell out of everything, *before* you make your move. Bet your ass that Buster was planning that move for most of the night, and you know that he waited for just the right moment when you weren't looking to pull it off. You didn't deserve that torte because you didn't want it as bad as he did. You weren't ready to go to the mat for it, but he was. Damn, I love that dog of mine."

Chapter 8

End Zone Networking

I returned from the South Pacific with a nice tan and an aggressive new attitude towards everything. I was ready to channel Tom Brickman and just destroy the job hunt; I would ruthlessly land my dream job by sheer force of iron will and total positive thinking. That was my approach for four months: ruthless and confident, completely focused on abundance and winning and self-empowerment.

But still, I had no job.

It's true that I had the attitude and swagger now, but unfortunately, there was still something missing; there was one more thing that I had to master before the universe would relent.

When I was a child, someone once told me that eighty percent of jobs are found through informal networking instead of formal job postings, and I really internalized that message, especially during the lean and mean teenage years. Networking helped me survive the *Lord of the Flies*-like social politics of middle school; it allowed me to completely dominate the middle tier of the high school chess team leadership (co-opting the old leadership and crushing a very well organized coup attempt), and it helped me totally defeat the unwitting substitute teacher who attempted to silence me during my in-class-stand-on-the-desk-Maori-War-Dance. I had the entire class chanting and beating their chests with face paint and fog machines. The substitute teacher ended up running from the building, never returning to education, unfortunately, but nobody said teaching was easy.

So I thought that I was quite the networking expert. But my job hunt proved otherwise. Despite my efforts to internalize the confidence and positivity of Tom Brickman, I just wasn't going anywhere all alone in my apartment, hiding under the bed, confidently sending off cover letters through the Internet, but not interacting with anybody who could tell how powerfully gleaming and supernatural I really was in person, under the bed.

I needed to make real connections; it was time to stop hiding and meet actual people who could help me find a real job. And for this, I would need to dust off my old networking skills, and make them even stronger. It was time to attend a networking conference.

The location was Scottsdale, Arizona. It was a recently built corporate office building with shiny marble, lush plants, waterfalls, and almond-smelling coffee shops in the expansively appointed beige and emerald green atrium. Outside it was pushing 95, but inside it was a pleasant 72 with low relative humidity. There were over a thousand people of all ages in business attire milling about hesitantly, engaging in idle small talk, waiting for the main event for which they had paid a considerable sum of money: the keynote address by Jedidiah Earl Lantern, a powerhouse in the crowded networking-empowerment community. A former Baptist minister, Lantern was a high-octane motivational speaker known for his conviction and creativity on the subject of networking. To some, networking was just another tool in the job-hunting universe, but to Lantern, networking was the golden chariot upon which you could fly to the heavens of your career ambitions, and catapult yourself around the sun at light speed until the vastness of the manifested galaxy was yours. And yet, tragically, nobody fully understood the awesome, untapped power of what Lantern referred to as *End Zone Networking*. And so it was his current mission in life to speak to the lost job-hunting people about this powerful and untapped resource.

We took our seats and prepared for the show. The lights dimmed and Lantern appeared behind the podium, looking down at us through the clouds with a warm, but ferocious look of utter concentration and relaxed poise. He was like an idling jet airliner just before turning onto the runway – calm and humming softly, but possessing a massive amount of power that yearned to break free of gravity, and take us all with him across the night skies.

"...You have come here today because you are desperate, and because you are tired." His voice reverberated throughout the banquet hall in a powerfully crisp and deliberate cadence. He had an awesome stage presence, with a relaxed confidence that could only be earned by life experience. "You have travelled here to this moment in time because you can no longer live with the sorry reflection of your past state of consciousness, and the repeated failures that continue to appear in your life, time and time again. You're sick and tired of the gray emptiness of not loving your life or your work – you are ready for change. For many of you it has been a rough and sorry road. But, my friends, the external change that you seek – the job and the dream career that you so strongly desire – will only come to you after, and only after, you have changed from within. And there is no way around that hard, rock-bottom truth."

I was struck by two things: first, what he was saying was true; and second, I wasn't sure how it related to networking.

"That's right, my friends, many of you will find that your orientation – your very disposition in this job hunt – is entirely backwards!!" He pounded his fist on the lectern and paused to stare intently at several people in the front row, who looked away from him. "…It is backwards because you are looking for a job. It is backwards because you are looking for a career! And no, this is not how things work! You only go looking for something that you do not have, and I am here to tell you that you have to live as if you already have your dream career – you have to believe deep down with every fiber of your being that you've already got everything that you want and need; it just hasn't showed up in your life yet. But it's out there waiting for you to claim it! You have to *imagine* it, and you have to *feel* it, as if it's already there. And once you understand this – and I mean when you really take this to heart – it will forever change how you approach what we call your 'job hunt,' and it will fundamentally change how you approach the people that you meet along the way. And when you totally and unapologetically embrace a higher version of yourself every single day – when you become the person that already has exactly what it is that you desire – then I know that miracles will happen. I know this to be true like I know that the sun will rise tomorrow morning."

I was intrigued. I had heard all this before, of course, but there was something about the way he said it. Something in his tone and the fiery look in his eyes that made me stop and seriously consider if maybe I had been too quick to dismiss this idea of visualization. He really, really believed what he was saying. It was infectious.

He continued, his voice growing in amplitude and passion. "You must decide what kind of life you want to lead – you must decide exactly what kind of career you want – and then you have to become that person prior to the career unfolding. You must align your internal energy to the external reality that you wish to see, and then – and only then – will those two realities come into harmony in your everyday life.

But I promise you: the internal shift happens before the external situation changes."

"That's right," I heard a man next to me agreeing with Lantern. The crowd was paying rapt attention to him; his words were strong enough, but his stage presence was something to behold – a human jetliner.

"...So if you want to grow fruit, you better tend to your own garden first! Fruit doesn't just show up because the gardener went looking for it! Because somebody gave it to him! No, my friends, it has to grow naturally and slowly from within the soil itself – by the undying optimism and hard, daily, nasty, unrelenting toil of the gardener who believes that the fruits are already present within the smallest of seeds. He believes and he trusts and he just knows deep down that those fruits are going to show themselves when the winter casts aside its bitter blanket, and so he works day in and day out, and time and time again until the sunshine cometh in the springtime, until those fruits appear. But he doesn't expect the fruit when his garden isn't ready; he has patience and fortitude, and he works on that garden like a soul obsessed at the crossroads! And the devil himself can't block him out from tending his garden. There is no power on earth that's going to block this man out! He will work his own garden until his fingers bleed and his soul cries out for water and the angry cold of winter melts under his hot and hungry will. And you just have to be that way with your dreams – work like your very life depended on it – make yourself powerful – be the better version of yourself that you know you can be. Visualize the result that you want – and work, work, work, work like a spirit unbroken, and you will know success!"

He paused to wipe the sweat from his brow and take a sip of ice water.

"...But I'm not talking about just fame and fortune here; that's low success – selfish success. I'm talking about the success of your higher self. Imagine that unique gift that only you can give to the world; imagine that gift coming forth from you and your labor, going out into the world and enriching other people's lives in an authentic way. Believe that your imagination for higher success is possible and true, and then watch as inspired action flows to you, and from you, naturally.

You'll just want to get up and work hard, because the ideas of what you need to do are so crystal clear in your head, that you're just getting out of the way, and letting those inspired ideas flow through you. And so, if you believe – and I mean, really, really, believe – and then you allow yourself to feel that excited inspiration that compels inspired action – then your dream career will have no choice but to rise from the ashes of a long dead, forgotten dream and bear real, sweet, precious fruit. I promise you the fruit will come! Thank the heavens above, the fruit will come to thee!"

"Amen! Say it again!" People shouted.

"...So, my friends, we have two very simple requirements for success: a fierce clarity of vision and a monster load of hard work. Put those two things together, and you are *unstoppable*. And so why don't we see more people doing this? Why don't we see more unstoppable people on our morning commutes or at our workplaces? Where are all the unstoppable people hiding? Everybody says they want to be successful – and it's no big secret how you get there – so why aren't more people successful? I'll tell you why: self-discipline.

Because if you don't have self-discipline, then all the intelligence and talent and passion and visualization in the world won't matter one bit. This, my friends, is where the rubber meets the road in terms of your dreams coming true. This is what divides the folks who will spend their lives in quiet desperation doing a job they don't like, and the folks who will prosper and shine radiantly in a career that they love. Self-discipline! That is what it all comes down to! Say this with me, now: I have more than enough self-discipline!"

"I have more than enough self-discipline!!" A thousand people shouted together in unison, including me.

"I am in command of my own destiny because I honor my promises to myself! Say it with me now!"

We all repeated the sentence with firm passion and clarity of voice.

"...Because any fool can have a vision – any fool can tell you that they love something. Any fool can tell you they have passion. But unless you have the self-discipline to actually walk the walk – well, then you may as well go home because you're wasting your time."

"So, when you make a promise to yourself – I don't care how small that promise is – you absolutely must keep that promise – because your dream depends upon you keeping that promise right now. And this doesn't come easy to people, so the key is to start small, and build up your 'promise-muscles.' Prove to yourself that you can honor your promises in the small things, and then over time, you will build your self-confidence and self-reliance to know that you will keep your promises to yourself in the big things and the very smallest of things, and *that is where dreams are made – they come alive when you honor your promises*." He paused, allowing silence to fill the hall, before continuing.

"...And so next time you make a to-do list and you tell yourself that you're going to do something – I don't care how small; it could be just taking out the garbage – you better believe you're going to keep that promise like your most important dream depends on it, because it does. I don't care if it's raining, or snowing, or if there's angry winds and hungry wolves, or if you're just plain dog-tired and you don't feel like it. No! Unacceptable! Go home! If you can't trust yourself to take out the garbage like you told yourself you would, well then – the game's over right there. Your dream is dead. Because you've got no credibility – you've got no self-discipline, and you're going nowhere fast. And so, I'm telling you now, if your to-do list includes taking out the garbage, then you better make sure you take out the garbage that day, no matter what. I said NO MATTER WHAT – do you hear me? I don't care if you have to crawl on your belly in the middle of a rainstorm when you're tired and hungry – you will take out the garbage that day like your life depends on it. Because it does."

"Take out the garbage! Yes sir!" A man shouted from behind me.

"And once that garbage is outside your house, like you promised yourself it would be, then you have kept the most important promise you'll ever make – the promise to yourself – and you have built your promise-muscles for the next time, when the challenge is greater, and the payoff is bigger. And this is how dreams are made. Step by step. Promise by promise. Commitment by commitment."

"That's right! Promises make the dream!" Someone else shouted exuberantly. It could've all been very cheesy, except that it really wasn't.

Lantern used his blue, silk handkerchief to wipe away more sweat from his brow before continuing in his deep, baritone voice. "Now, you all are probably wondering – what's all this got to do with networking? Well, I'll tell you. Networking is about how you relate to other people – that's it. And how you relate to other people is above all else a reflection of how you relate to yourself. If you honor yourself, and you keep your promises to yourself, and you take care of yourself, then you will exude power, dignity, and honor, and people are going to sense that. And you will wind up meeting other people who respect themselves – because you won't be able to abide anything less; you won't have time for the complainers or the lazy folks who bring you down with their negativity. You don't need to be around that kind of energy, and you're not going to want to be around that type of energy, once you honor yourself. And when you surround yourself with people who inspire you – people who excite you and challenge you, rather than drag you down – then opportunities and challenges and excitement will flow to you naturally, because that's the environment of empowered people. People who respect themselves are empowered people. So begin to respect yourself right now, and join the ranks of the empowered! That's what networking can be!"

Lantern took a deep swig of bottled water. He was giving it his all.

"Now, let me tell you what networking is not! There are a lot of myths out there about networking because it's such a big and powerful thing and people don't really understand it properly, so all these myths have grown up around it, and I am here to break down and defeat those myths, so that you can embrace the potentiality of what networking can be for you. I want you to experience the best of what networking can be! Repeat after me: Networking is what I make of it!"

Everybody repeated the sentence loudly and clearly.

"...Now, there are people who will tell you that networking is shady or opportunistic. It's phony and cheap. Well now, if you expect it to be that way, then yes, it will be that way. But it will only be phony and cheap if you approach it that way, and if you do it that way, then I guarantee that you will invite phony and cheap experiences into your life. So, don't do it that way!! Now, repeat after me: 'I will only network with integrity because I am a person of integrity!'"

A thousand people made a promise to themselves to network with integrity.

"That's right – it's up to you to define how your networking will go. It all comes back to your relationship with yourself: if you respect yourself, then you will invite others who respect themselves into your life, and networking will be a beautiful thing. But if you don't respect yourself, then you'll invite others who don't respect themselves into your life, and you'll be networking from a place of disrespect and desperation, and there is nobody who wants that. So, don't do it!"

"Yes sir!" We shouted back.

"Now, why is networking so important? What about experience or writing a good resume or having a great interview? Why don't I talk about those things more? Well, I'll tell you why – those things all matter, but networking is the golden key: networking is where possibilities are made! Networking is the pumped up amplifier in the job hunt. Think back on all your life experiences; think about where you've lived or jobs that you've had. What do you think about first? It's the people, right? You think about the people! How many of you said, 'people,' raise your hands!"

Almost all of the hands in the audience went up.

"People are the stitches in the fabric of your dreams! They are the first, second and third bases in the game of life! What do winners at the Academy Awards do first? They thank people! What do best-selling authors do in the beginning of their book? They acknowledge the people who made the book possible. What do you need when you apply for a job? You need recommendations from other people. You just can't achieve your dreams without the help of other people, so you need to make sure you have a good relationship with the people who come into your life, personally and professionally. Don't network with people who you don't respect! Nothing good will come of that, I promise you! But don't respect people so that they can help you win an Oscar or get a book published! No! That's backwards! You will naturally respect people when you respect yourself. When self-respect becomes your language and your way of operating – then you can't help but respect other people who deserve your respect. Are you hearing me?"

"Yes we are!!"

"And how do you learn the language of self-respect? You learn it day in and day out, with every little promise that you keep to yourself – that's how you learn it!"

Lantern paused again to take a breath and let the words sink in.

"So, there are two kinds of networking. There's what I call *End Zone Networking*, which is what we've been talking about; it's powerful networking built on respect and integrity. And then there's *Red Zone Networking*, which is the opposite; it's based on desperation and opportunism and fear. Now, let me tell you a story about a friend of mine that illustrates how most people are doing it wrong. Most people are using *Red Zone Networking*, and they just aren't seeing results, and they don't know why, because *Red Zone Networking* is what most people are teaching at these job-hunting conventions and in those job-hunting books – they're all talking about this type of networking, and it doesn't work – it only keeps you in the red zone, not the end zone, which is where you want to be! So I'm going to tell you a story that will teach you how to go from red zone to end zone."

Lantern was overflowing with enthusiasm and passion. He couldn't wait to tell us about *End Zone Networking*. And we couldn't wait to hear about it.

"So, my good friend Eddie was out there looking for a job as a professional chef, and he called me up one day, and said, 'Jed, you know I've been networking now for two months, sending out emails to people, calling my friends, looking up old college connections, using social media, asking around, and nothing is going my way. What am I doing wrong?' And so we started talking, and it turns out that Eddie was very deeply entrenched in the habit of *Red Zone Networking*. What I mean by this is that he was desperate for a touchdown, and he felt like it was the 4th quarter of his job hunt, and he was ready to throw a Hail Mary to just about anybody who was open – so he was projecting all this desperation out into the world. So that type of desperation is the first element of *Red Zone Networking*, but there's something else, which is the second defining characteristic of the red zone. It's habitual – when teams get into the red zone, they have a habit of falling back on the same old tired plays that they've been using all season, and not trying anything new! Teams don't want to experiment when they're in the red zone because they're nervous! Now, Eddie didn't realize it, but he was only networking with his current social and professional network – the people he already knew, or the people who knew those people. But, basically, he was just repeating the same old plays with his same old people, or their same old people!"

Lantern paused for a moment and smiled at the audience. He wasn't nervous at all, just emanating contentedness and calm.

"...Now, you might be thinking: 'what's wrong with networking within my current social and professional network? Who else am I going to network with? Total strangers? How do I do that?' Well, there's nothing wrong with networking in your current social and professional network if you don't want to see any real change in your life. But if you want to see substantial change in your life, then you need to stop focusing on the same old people! When you interact only with the friends and coworkers who are in your life right now, you're just going to get more of the same. Even friends of friends – coworkers of coworkers or associates of associates who you don't know – well, the chances are that these folks are going to be very similar to the friends and coworkers that you already have. Why? Because people tend to surround themselves with other people who are very similar to them – people in the same energy groove. So, you're just going to keep bumping into the same types of people if you limit your networking to your current associates or even their associates! And that's how you never reach the end zone! Because most people aren't in the end zone! They're in the red zone, going back and forth with the other team all day, doing things the way they've always done them, but never moving the ball into the end zone – never realizing their dreams! Never loving their jobs! Most folks are just getting by! And if you're tired of that type of desperate situation, then you need to network with people who are already in the end zone! These are the people who are already doing what you want to be doing! They love their jobs, and they love their lives, and they're passionate people! You need to go out and meet them, and learn from them! Experience a different way of being in the world than what you are used to! You want to get ripped? Then go down to the gym and seek out a group of people who are already ripped, and spend a lot of time with these ripped folks, and pretty soon you'll be on your way to having six pack abs! Do you hear what I'm saying? If you want to be a professional actor, then you need to meet other people who are already professional actors – get to know them! Learn from them! Learn from whatever it is they're doing right! It's their energy state that you need to be around! You're not going to find that type of energy in a book – you need to feel it in the flesh of real life! Now, it's true, you might not be able to meet these folks personally; maybe you don't know anybody who knows any professional actors or ripped body builders, but that's okay because you can meet them! Take a class; go to the gym; travel; get outside your comfort zone, and pretty soon you will meet new and exciting people, some of whom will already be doing the things that you yourself would like to be doing. And when you meet them, you'll learn how they got where they are now. That's *End Zone Networking*! Now, you can start this type of networking even before you have the opportunity to travel – before you've had the opportunity to meet new and exciting people. How? Just use the Internet! Read books! Watch interviews! Expose yourself to the type of energy you want to be around! So let's say you want to be a musician, but you don't know anybody who is one, and you can't afford to travel or take a music class taught by a professional musician. Well, just spend an hour a day online watching interviews and classes and speeches by actual, real-life musicians, and you will expose yourself to their energy in a positive way. That's virtual *End Zone Networking*, and it still works!"

People in the audience were nodding along, watching Lantern intensely. He was very much in the end zone, moving smoothly about the stage, his body language natural, relaxed, and accessible.

"So, getting back to my friend, Eddie. Well, he wanted to be a professional chef in a gourmet restaurant, but his only experience had been working as an assistant cook in a fast food restaurant. Now, if you've ever sampled Eddie's cooking, you know he's got the skills. My boy can cook! Gumbo, Cajun, French, Tex-Mex, Thai, Indian…Eddie can do it all, and he really loves food like nobody's business. But, Eddie's got a problem because he knows he can cook gourmet with the best of them, but nobody in the top tier gourmet restaurants in town knows that he can cook, so what's he going to do? His friends and his coworkers don't know anybody at the best restaurants, because most of them are also working at fast food restaurants or they're working in retail or serving at chain restaurants. So you see that his professional circle did not include the big shots at the finest restaurants in town – the folks who could give him his dream job. And so Eddie was going nowhere fast with his job hunt, and as we were talking, I explained to him about *End Zone Networking*, and what that would mean for him. It meant that Eddie would have to stop looking for his dream job among the people that he already knew, or the people that they already knew. He needed to push his comfort level, and get to know some other gourmet chefs! And when I told Eddie this, a light bulb just went on, like it was so obvious, but yet – he wasn't doing it! Very few people are doing it, because you have to step outside your comfort box."

"So, how did Eddie finally get into the end zone? Well, first he started watching online videos every night with gourmet chefs talking about their craft, and then he started getting book ideas from these videos, and then those books gave him some inspired ideas about ways that he could improve his technique with *Gambas al Ajillo* – it's a type of Spanish Tapas, and one of his favorite foods to prepare – and so Eddie signed up for a class about Spanish Tapas techniques, and pretty soon, Eddie's surrounded with gourmet chefs every week at this class, and he's talking with them about cooking techniques, and they're becoming his friends, and they can feel his passion, and they can see his skills, and they don't care that he's only worked at fast food joints, because they've seen how Eddie can cook, and they like him because he's a good guy with integrity – does what he says he's going to do. And within three weeks, one of his classmates who worked at one of the finest restaurants in town is telling Eddie how he's moving to Spain, and he's asking Eddie if he'd like to apply for his current job! And so, pretty soon, Eddie's got an interview at this gourmet restaurant, and one of the interviewers is his same friend from the class! And so Eddie's got the job! His dream job! Like it's nothing! It just happened so easily, once he put himself into the circle of the right people. And this can work for you too!"

People started clapping.

"Now, the important thing about this story of my friend Eddie – you'll notice that Eddie didn't use anybody; he didn't manipulate anybody or pretend to be anything that he's not. He networked in the end zone with total sincerity! Sure, he wanted to land his dream job, and that was definitely a reason for taking the class, but he also took the class because he genuinely loves to cook, and he had the inspired idea of honing his skills with Spanish Tapas – so, it was just a side benefit that he met someone who could help him get closer to his dreams. And he made friends naturally in this class, not because he wanted something from them, but because he just liked the people in the class. It was a merger of sincerity and opportunity. That's *End Zone Networking!*"

Lantern grinned at us all from the stage and pumped his fist in the air several times.

"So, I leave you with these four things, and they will change your life if you apply them correctly: vision, hard work, self-discipline, and *End Zone Networking*. Have a vision – and a conviction in the reality of that vision – that is so clear that it moves you to action: ferocious and inspired action! Then, practice total self-discipline, which means that you keep the promises that you make to yourself in the little things and the big things. And finally, don't network with the same old people and their same old network – No!! Get out there and meet new people and expose yourself to new ideas and new energies! Surround yourself with the energy that you want to inhabit within yourself. Do all four of these things, and you will be unstoppable! I promise you, your life will begin to actually change from the inside out, and your sweet dreams will finally be within your reach!" Lantern pumped his fist and dove into the audience like a rock star, with the crowd carrying him on their shoulders and chanting, "*End Zone! End Zone! End Zone!*"

Two days after the networking conference, I finally started to take out the garbage. Three weeks later, I began taking classes in photography again for the first time since college. Eight weeks later, I had met three successful professional photographers. Three months later, I had lined up my first interview for a part-time position as a staff photographer for an advertising agency. While that interview ultimately didn't work out, I had never gotten so close to the end zone, and I knew it wouldn't be long before I would score the game-winning touchdown.

Chapter 9

The 9 Job Hunting Keys

After returning from the networking conference, I sat down to write everything I had learned thus far, during my job hunt. Here are the key takeaways:

1. HR People are looking for obvious story arcs in your resume and cover letter, and if your life is a bit messy, and non-linear, you might have some trouble.

As someone who majored in mechanical engineering, only to pursue a career as a professional photographer after college, I sympathize with those who have changed majors, or careers, once or twice. Many of us are not born with a single, all-consuming desire to pursue a specific career, which we plan and implement strategically from the age of twelve onwards. And many of us also change our priorities and values, as we grow and develop as people. The person that I am now hardly resembles the person that I was in college, when I declared my major and set certain things in motion, and I think that's a good thing. But be advised – the advice from HR people is that your resume and cover letter should tell a story that is logical, tidy, overarching and inevitably trending towards that one particular job to which you're applying right now, in an almost cosmically consonant way: "Ah, I see you've always been fascinated with user-interface design – wonderful! Your resume shows that you were the president of the user-interface club in your junior high school, and you helped design the friendliest interface for children's video games while you were still in high school! And since then, you've only taken classes in user interface design and children's video games! This is just what we want – someone who knows what they want – someone with a fierce clarity of vision! Someone with a ridiculously specific background that freakishly matches our impossibly stringent job posting! You're hired!"

So, if that's not you, don't give up hope. Your task is not impossible. You simply need to present your background in such a way that a sane person could see a tenable way in which your undergraduate degree in anthropology helped to prepare you for this job as a back-end web developer. It's not impossible. But you should be aware that you're up against a cultural bias that often penalizes people for changing their minds, and fails to recognize the concept of multiple or transferrable intelligence. So, be creative when you craft your job application; and above all, try and find a coherent thread that weaves it all together, and which makes it seem inevitable that you would be applying for this job now, as if it's the logical denouement of your education and work experience. Because it seems that almost everyone in HR is looking for that thread, whether it's fair or not.

2. Unpaid (or paid) Internships are a critical way of breaking into an industry.

If you can swing it, unpaid internships are extremely valuable for getting your foot in the door. How do you get an internship? You usually have to be in college or graduate school, and of course you have to be in a situation where you're able to work for free, so obviously this fact benefits those with financial means. While they have been criticized as being exploitive and of course benefitting the wealthy, they do provide job seekers with a way to break into an industry with no prior experience in that field, and the opportunity to make a solid impression on a prospective employer. While it's no secret that internships can be helpful for these reasons, the fact that they are so dependent upon being a student doesn't get enough attention. Many organizations won't accept interns unless they are full-time students, so if you are a student, take advantage of this golden opportunity, and go find an internship (usually unpaid) in the field that you're most interested in working someday. College professors and administrators are sometimes shielded from the harsh realities of job-hunting in the wild frontier, so they might not sell these internships to their students as strongly as they could. But if you're a student, this is a really powerful opportunity. You might never be a student again; here's your chance to grab an internship. And don't wait for an internship to be advertised; contact the organization that you're most interested in, and ask them if they have any internships available.

3. *Your confidence will drop. Talk with friends. Stay connected.*

No matter how strong you are, you will get rattled from being without work. If you're job hunting while you currently have a job – that's great. That was good planning on your part. But if you're not in that situation, it's going to get stressful. Getting up in the morning and going to a job gives people so much: purpose, dignity, motion, and a sense of contribution. Now, if you're a Zen master, you obviously know that your essential identity as a spiritual being has nothing to do with your job. But how many of us are Zen masters? It definitely helps to have a job. And when you don't have a job, you're very much in danger of losing that sense of connection to society, and to your immediate community. So, the best solution is to rediscover that connection: seek out your friends, and talk to them about what you're experiencing. And of course, talk to other job hunters. If you can't find them, read online message boards and online support groups to remind yourself that you're not alone. Disconnection is dangerous; don't let yourself go down that dark path via self-pity or dramatic narratives about how special and sad you are. There are other people who are experiencing exactly what you're experiencing right now. Always keep that in mind. You're not alone in this stressful experience.

4. *Don't rush it.*

Here's the irony: the more that you resist the state of being without work, the worse it will be. Obviously you want this experience to be over as soon as possible. But the more you complain about it and fight it, the worse it becomes. If you accept it fully, you let go of the painful resistance and tension that drains you of the energy that is required for effective action. Try to accept that this is where you are right now, and let yourself experience that reality without judgment or self-pity; effective action will arise from a place of peace, not desperate resistance. Of course, it's hard to be without work, but this state of unemployment doesn't say anything about you as a person; rather, it says something about the harsh nature of our new globalized economy, where countless jobs have been eliminated by technology and outsourcing. Accept the state of being without work, and try and relax into the job hunt, and know that it will take some time.

And right now you might be saying, "But I don't have the luxury of time. I don't have enough money in savings to simply embrace the situation, and settle into it! I need a job ASAP! The rent is due!" I totally understand that reality, but if you let that panicked desperation seep into your mentality, it will weaken you and undermine your efforts to change your situation for the better. It's like with dating – if you walk around feeling desperate and needy, and projecting that vibe out into the world, you're not going to be attractive to anyone. Find peace with where you are first, and then effective action towards finding a job will arise from you more powerfully and organically, without being tainted by anger and desperation.

5. *Savings, Savings, Savings*.

Enough said. You absolutely need it to sustain yourself during the experience. Without it, you'll need to find a temporary job in order to support yourself while looking for a better job. Savings allows you to skip that intermediate step, and to focus on finding that better job. Granted, you might not have any money in savings on account of the ridiculously high cost of living and stagnant middle class wages. I hear you. There are no simple answers here, and we're dealing in a twisted circular logic: you need a temporary job in order to support yourself while looking for a good job because it can take months to find a good job, but sometimes it's hard just to find that temporary job, so you need to rely on savings. But you don't have any savings because your last job wasn't a good job, so now you need to find another bad job in order to find a better job because your last job wasn't a good job. Frustrating.

6. *College is both the key and the chain.*

We have an unsustainable social arrangement right now: college is the key to finding a good job, but the exorbitant student loans required for college are the chains that bind us and drain us of our energies during our working lives. You essentially have to sell your working soul into student loan debt in order to obtain a job that will simply allow for a living wage. Look for more vocational alternatives to college in the not too distant future. In the meantime, be a wise consumer before spending upwards of $200,000 on a four-year degree; make sure that the skills you acquire during those four years will actually translate into a job. And remember how much each class is costing you, if you're ever tempted to cut class, or give anything less than your best effort. This is not high school; you're spending enough money to buy a small house to acquire the skills for your career – make the most of it. And that includes doing an internship.

7. *Don't play roles. Everybody can sense inauthenticity.*

One of the worst things you can do during your job hunt is to subordinate your intuitive sense of what to say and do to some expert's advice about what you should say and do. There are some job hunting books and websites out there that will actually tell you how much eye contact to make during an interview, and how firm your handshake should be, and how many minutes to spend on each response. Please – don't become a robot. It's a cliché, I know, but it's a cliché for a reason: just be yourself. It works. Being inauthentic and robotic never works. We're all pretty much the same, and everybody understands that you're a little nervous during a job hunt. Remember that the HR people want to hire you, because they have a job to do too. They're really just looking for people that they can imagine themselves working with, so just relax, and treat your interviewers as you would a coworker. Be nice, normal, and human, and stop thinking about whether you're making a good impression, or how many seconds of eye contact is appropriate. All that stuff is a distraction.

As someone who has interviewed my fair share of real people, I can attest that when someone is playing a role, treating me as an abstraction rather than as another human being, it creates a wall between us, and it makes the whole experience of interviewing very fake and unpleasant. Just be authentic. Really.

8. *Minimize expenses to maximize freedom.*

If you're someone who wants to work 60 hours a week climbing the corporate ladder with a massive salary, a giant house and a frazzled lifestyle, that's totally your prerogative, and I respect that. To each his own. But if you're someone who's deeply passionate about something that doesn't necessarily pay that well, such as: music, dance, photography, teaching, writing, acting, exercise, etc., then you have to face up to this basic equation that dominates our lives:

More Stuff = Less Time

We all work for different reasons, but obviously a huge part of getting a job is earning an income. And our incomes pay for our stuff. If you don't need as much stuff, then you don't need as much income, and you own more of your time. So, if you want time to do things that don't necessarily pay the bills, then think seriously about how much stuff you actually need before applying for that all-consuming high-octane job.

9. *What you're looking for might not be out there. It might be in you.*

A lot of people are unhappy with their jobs, and there are a lot of crazy structures in our society that make our jobs unfulfilling and inefficient. While some people are lucky to find a niche within those structures, many of us don't mesh with the traditional 9–5 office job format, and no clever job search will ever change that reality. If what you're looking for isn't out there, maybe it's time to build it for yourself. It's no easy task, of course, but it's also not very easy to spend your adult life in a job that doesn't inspire you, working for someone else. We live in an incredibly exciting time, filled with opportunity and innovation. The internet is a great equalizer, and the tools that you need to start your own venture are all within your reach. All you need is the motivation and a relentless work ethic. We are a nation of entrepreneurs, and there's no reason we have to settle for anything less than a passionate and fulfilling career that we create for ourselves, by the force of our own iron will.

Epilogue

Two weeks after completing this book, I landed a part-time job as a staff photographer for an online magazine, using the principles I learned from the Lantern networking speech in Arizona. I work a second job in a coffee shop to make ends meet, and I spend my early mornings and evenings developing my own freelance photography business. I'm not in the end zone yet, but I'm closing in fast.

All the knowledge in every job-hunting book (including this one) – all the strategies and tactics and formulas – they don't mean anything unless you're hungry enough for real change – unless you're truly sick and tired of just getting by in a job that 'could be worse.'

And now, please excuse me, but I have to go take out the garbage. Because I promised myself I would.

Made in the USA
Middletown, DE
05 June 2019